ADVANCE PRAISE

"In this empowering guide, the award-winning Najjar offers an extraordinary life approach to reach new heights as he lays out strategies for turning negative beliefs and ideas into positive ones.... this is a book that can change your life. Najjar has delivered a winner."

—The Prairies Book Review

"The You Beyond You: The Knowledge Of The Willing by Ramzi Najjar is a profound and thought-provoking book that helps readers look at unfolding the secrets of living life to its utmost potential."

—Readers' Favorite

"I recommend this motivational book to anyone who is on a journey of self-discovery. The YOU Beyond you is written for people who are ready to elevate beyond a personal level of consciousness to understanding the collective consciousness better."

—Literary Titan

"In The YOU beyond you - The knowledge of the willing, Ramzi Najjar addresses his audience with the contemplative calm of a mystic guru and the fervor of an old-time evangelist, in a how-to guide to good health, happiness, and inner peace as a personal philosophic treatise addressing the physical and spiritual quality of life in the 21st century."

—Chanticleer Book Reviews

"Presenting a compelling and optimistic approach towards living one's best life, The YOU Beyond You is both a philosophical and practical guide to enlightenment and self-improvement. Najjar combines his personal experiences and spiritual theories for a uniquely inspiring read."

—Self-Publishing Review

"The You Beyond You: The Knowledge of the Willing by Ramzi Najjar is a book of motivational nonfiction that endeavors to transform lives. In its pages, Najjar proves to be a diligent thinker as well as an assiduous and clear communicator about topics that might just spark change within. The You Beyond You is a gift that can show you the way"

—Independent Book Review

The **YOU** beyond you

The **YOU** beyond you

THE KNOWLEDGE OF THE WILLING

RAMZI NAJJAR

Anecdote
Publishing House

Anecdote
Publishing House

Anecdote Publishing House
E-35-A, E Block, Gali No. 2 Ganesh Nagar,
Pandav Nagar Complex Delhi-110092

Published by Anecdote Publishing House

First Edition 2021

ISBN 978-81-952518-0-3

MRP ₹250

Book Promoted and Marketed by Champ Readers Pvt. Ltd.
Edited by Mansi Narula Kashyap
Layout and Cover by Graphic Tailor
Printed by Thomson Press (India) Ltd, New Delhi

Dedication

'This book is dedicated to my daughter Vanessa, with the hope that she will grasp the material provided herein and model her life accordingly.
It is published as a return of appreciation to my parents, my family and the Universe, who all contribute to the person that I am.

CONTENT

PREFACE

In a chaotic world, and a life of prevalent restlessness, how can we make sense of the nonsensical?

Though the notion may sound far fetched, the reality remains that this is our current state of being. The world we live in has certainly progressed to untold levels, but it has also rendered us oblivious to our well-being and the pollutants we unwittingly allow into our lives.

Through this book, I will attempt to unfold the secrets of living life to its utmost potential, whilst still allowing those that seek balance to celebrate the benefits the world has to offer. This book I believe will offer a lengthy discussion on the dynamics of life, their nature and how they operate.

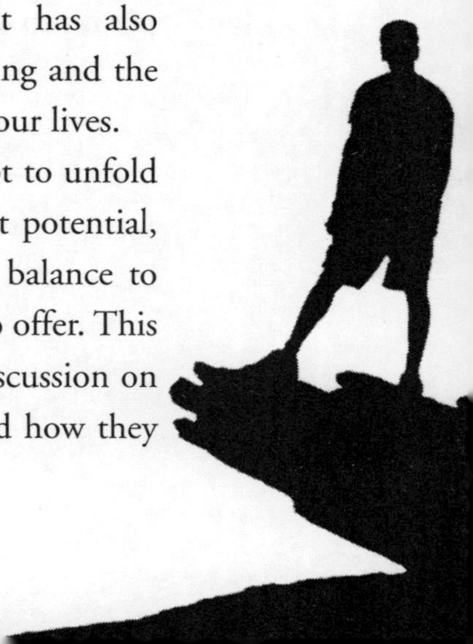

This will not be an easy endeavor as it attempts to relay a state of living that goes beyond words and expressions.

While reading this book, you will get to know about how some of our daily routine habits debase the true value of life.

As you dive into this enlivening account of my experiences, you will realize, as I did, that more often than not, it is not the world around us that is to be blamed for the quality of the life we live, it is our approach towards life that determines the quality of living, as well as what we allow to become a part of it.

I will also attempt to cross-check with scientific evidence the concepts which I believe form our reality, that differs greatly from that which is always being perceived.

"In essence, it can be summed up to one idea: you become what you perceive…and what you permit to enter your body."

INTRODUCTION

I can still recall 'the day' I turned off the television at my office, and looked outside the window across the street, where people were walking back and forth. While my gaze lingered, I thought about how to dispel the growing unease that I was experiencing? Expatiating the reasons and causes, I realized at that very moment, that watching massacres unfold in different parts of the world on the news was primarily responsible for my nagging discomfort. This instilled a prior conviction that the news' negativity was essentially the main contributor to any bleak thoughts or sensations I felt.

I returned home, and, for the first time, was confronted with how I was living my life.

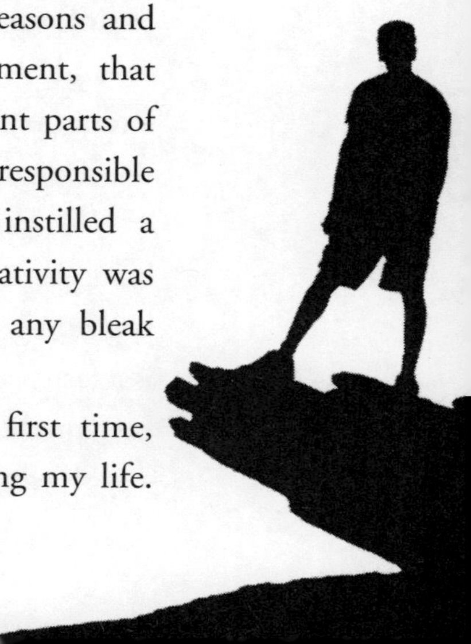

I wondered why I had been subjecting myself to such constant negativity, only to come home feeling drained.

I made a conscious decision that day not to watch TV the day that follows. And as expected, my experience was going smoother and better in all directions. That was the last time I watched any TV program, and the first day I gave up what I had attributed as a regular mode of living. A more conscious approach was needed to strive in the environment I lived in. Being exposed to a multitude of experiences, as well as constantly being bombarded with information meant that I needed to analyze the underlying biological and psychological factors in order to establish my way of living, and consequently, my identity.

We amass endless hours of education and knowledge through the years to try to assemble all the pieces of the puzzle, and make something out of our lives. We try to cope up with people around us, as well as our surroundings. We seldom try, however, to comprehensively analyze our thoughts and actions.

We rarely take our failures, and state of being as a stop sign to return to the point of beginning. We think fast and act faster, and as it is a fast-paced world we live in, we are constantly pressured to keep up.

Slowing down the pace is necessary to

align our thoughts, and experiences, and draw constructive conclusions and adequate solutions.

Every event, every experience, teaches us a life lesson. We only need to clear our minds and adopt a method of questioning to extract these lessons. What we ultimately need to instill in our lives is the curiosity within us to research and analyze matters.

One should be reawakened to who they really are and reach a more authentic version of themselves. "When we dive deeper into these life lessons, a whole new world is unveiled, and soon enough, our place in this unlimited Universe is aligned."

Humans are fated to win in one instance, and fail in another. These are rules when getting involved in any life experience, especially if we are tackling new grounds. Our failure determines our persistence.

To pick ourselves up, and try again is the real driving force behind success. When one falls in life, it must be ascertained that one has something solid to build on, rather than just reconstructing on debris.

Many of us advance through an age without gaining insight into the problems we are faced with. Few of us have grasped that issues happen for a reason, and every situation is a blessing in itself. This can only be understood if one analyzes recent occurrences for as long as it is required to draw adequate conclusions, and move on.

Determining life lessons on the spot is an impossibility. The best method to learn the most from it, is to relinquish the thought of it with faith that it was for one's best interest. As life goes through different phases, it leaves us little clues here and there that allow us to extract the hidden meanings. The greatest lesson I learned so far is that what was most important was not the problem, but rather what I was going to do about it.

Reality exists within us, and so does prosperity, abundance, happiness, and success. However, we have learned to lead a life of limitation, expecting Only validation from the outside. Stuck in the social framework and idiosyncratic constructs, we lead very restricted lives, not allowing ourselves to become truly aware of this fact. Governments, societies, teachings, and our families have all set boundaries for us, that keep us entangled.

We are currently living our lives in survival mode, thus in fight or flight modes. This mental state's virulence results in consequent aggression, chaos, and uncertainty that only lead us to unpleasantness and always feeling like something is missing.

The quantity of information we are bombarded with, both positive or negative, is over-flooding our minds with pictures and outside stimuli from all sides irrespective of what we wish for and the direction we choose to take. Whilst the desire to take our life in a given order exists, our brain is confused by the external factors that offer a wide array of choices that get registered in our unconscious mind.

"We wonder thus through life, living it unconsciously, and expect a better outcome for our future."

We have become machines of 220V that are plugged into a 440V power supply. Consequently, disaster ensues.

Only a few of us are able to unlock and benefit from the power of mental clarity. Single-mindedness, singular focus, clarity of perception, and freedom of thought are the true gifts for successful living.

The reality is that we are enslaving ourselves, and holding our capabilities hostage. Our body, and passive mind that act as captors. We are trapped in the illusion of mindful freedom. This is a mirage when we are actually subjected to a stream of preconditioning, from all corners to the extent that we are unable to realize the constraint our perspective has become.

"It is only by breaking free of this conditioning, and unwillingly amassed bad habits that we can nurture curiosity and learning."

This child-like curiosity enables us to fully achieve what we seek to accomplish. "No one should expect a caged lion to rule the jungle."

Creating giant tornadoes around us and regularly jumping in and out of them through a multitude of actions is not the solution. What we need to establish is a path we can abide by. We can either decide to actively lead more positive lives and remove all external stimuli, or remain conditioned to our misery. A joyful life is built, not won in a competition.

There are rules for leading a good life, and rules mean preventing bad habits and desires.

Being torn between what we desire and what we want is a heavy burden. It is a truck loaded with more than its capacity going nowhere.

How do we win? One must first unload the unnecessary carriage, and achieve psychological maneuverability. These conflicting scenarios have transformed many of us into materialistic, self-centered individuals that are only concerned about their well-being.

We are unaware of the environment we strive in; we do not really grasp the fact that society also plays a significant role in our lives.

Reciprocity is essential; before receiving, one should give; nothing comes to us if we do not give an amount of it before. Accordingly, one must begin by implementing the logic of giving before receiving.

In life, the majority of us only expect to receive. We have become conditioned to only giving when receiving. However, "no man is an island entire of itself." If we did, we wouldn't be subjected to any societal pressure. Alone on this island, success and happiness wouldn't matter.

But when it comes to the lives we are leading; happiness sadly isn't achieved naturally.

The idea of constantly comparing ourselves with others compels us to feel like something is missing; especially constant exposure to social media, where everyone pictures themselves at their best, is widening.

We must concede to success, and all significant states of being, have no value unless we share them with those around us. Thinking about our success, and well-being is something that comes naturally. However, those thoughts should be reflected in our daily life in order to create a difference in the world. True joy lies in bettering the lives of others. By doing so, one can almost immediately notice positive improvements in one's own life.

The more we fail to notice this chain of events, the harder it would be to mark our personal growth as we narrow our social interactions against our own human nature.

The world around us today has been scaled

down to people hiding behind their phones. While all this relatively new technology is an essential means of communication and learning, it restricts our perspectives to narrow our existence pathways. These acts adversely affect our vision and true potential. We have, in many ways, disregarded connectivity amongst real people around us and have chosen to interact virtually, instead.

This mode of living has resulted in the creation of a world of images. We unwittingly elevate bubbles around ourselves, ultimately rendering our lives into prisons, and concentration camps, managed by our ingrained thinking patterns. With the constant feeling of emptiness, we eventually realize, "the how shallow" our lives have become.

We should redevelop a need for deeper interactions with others.

Some remain impervious, and maintain this pattern of living. Those that do eventually experience a sense of chaos as though they are sinking in the eye of a tornado. We have developed multiple realities in our heads while turning a blind eye towards our true selves. The ease with which we can access information might have served to amplify our knowledge, yet we remain unaware of the fundamental knowledge. We currently look to our environment only for validation. We are deeply taken by the material elements that surround us, that look very shiny from the outside, without giving real importance to establishing human ties. We have turned our minds into our worst enemies at a time where the mind is the doorway to a larger, more elaborate reality.

At that stage, our mind only can be the pathway to our freedom, and our salvation.

Suppressing our problems, and relishing the illusion of perfection, disables our ability to deal with living a real life. Maintaining a sense of utopic denial with a smiling façade is a dangerous psychological game that restricts our ability to live a healthy life. If these habits are carried on for too long, one would not be able to climb back the internal walls of the fake reality one created for himself.

Offered across the media, we have become conditioned to seeking out problems, accidents, murders, and general negativity. We enjoy binding ourselves to this negative reality, either for the sake of feeling alive or experiencing a hormonal rush. Being cognizant of negative realities adds to our sense of security, in a way, in knowing that it is happening outside our sphere. Unknowingly, it has become an effective way for the energy boost, creating distractions and routine disruption. This illusion, though, has very adverse effects on our wellbeing. What is real around us, as well as what is fake, has unilaterally become who we are. Our subconscious mind is conditioned to store and display whatever information it receives. The subconscious mind does not know how to differentiate between the two sensibilities.

For others, life has become a routine, a certain repetitiveness of waking up, killing time with work or other activities, and going to sleep without consciously evaluating the day that unfolded.

This consequently has disastrous effects on one's passive state of mind. Failing to impose a conscious direction, and a clear perception of what we want could trigger a vicious cycle of too many lags, where one tends to forget the past, passively agonizes about the present, and goes to sleep fearing the future.

If meticulous attention is given to our thoughts during the day, we might discover that the brain is limited to very few choices. We mainly focus on our daily tasks, problems, and consider this to be the norm by way of habituation without paying attention to our capabilities, and set of skills.

We have thus become small problem solvers as opposed to dreamers. We tend to focus on our daily routines to a crippling extent. The multitude of daily events and the fast-track life we all are leading creates a constant feeling of unease, fear, and remorse. The negative externalities in our daily lives impact our biological, spiritual, and psychological stability. We become more, and more distanced from our true purpose, and are carried away to create our tailored illusions. These transform into swamps where we drown in our negative thoughts, constantly wondering why life is so difficult, forgetting that we only need to swim to get to the shore.

The constant inflation and deflation of the bubbles we live in based on our everyday experiences and circumstances and the negativity we are being subjected to are shaping our characters, attitudes, and values. We, therefore, have unwillingly surrendered to the programming of the limitation, where success is an impossibility.

We thus aimlessly wander in circles instead of reaching our goals head-on. We have placed point A (our attitudes) inside one circle and point B (our goals and objectives) in another circle. Our brain is unable to grasp the existence of point B, or anything besides the circle we find ourselves in.

Most of us are living in comfort zones, not even psychologically allowing ourselves to explore the possibility of what really exists on the other side. We have preconditioned our brains to maintain our status just below our imagined breaking points, at a time where breaking points do not exist.

In effect, the possibilities available for us are unlimited. Once we decide to get out of our swamp and aim at a real direction in life, everything would become possible.

It is sometimes worth stepping back for several days in order to determine where one has reached in his life. What one has accomplished so far, and what one would like to amend?

When I personally embarked on that journey, I realized that my life wasn't even one percent of what I wanted it to be. I had taken too many paths rather than focusing on fewer productive ones. Thus, I decided to begin organizing my life and to set specific goals. Exercise is always a good starting point as it eases the pressures of the mind.

Soon after, I discovered that my body wasn't responding as it should. My second goal was to jot down all that comes to my mind and to revisit them later. At a glance, I could see that negativity prevailed, and that constituted a real shock. Still, the worst was the realization that what I thought I knew. I, in fact, knew only on a superficial level.

To gain knowledge up to this point, I mainly relied on my personal experiences, work, random discussions, and what reaches me on social media.

It is then that I realized I needed a complete overhaul of my entire life, my body, and my mind.

ONE

BODY POLLUTION

RETURNING TO EXERCISE was paramount. It was the most difficult beginning, since my body lacked the stamina it used to possess. My body became so accustomed to my lack of movement that any effort became uncomfortable. My body had gathered fat in places, and it weighed down on my movements. My breaths became shorter, which was something I hadn't expected to experience at my age.

After some time, I began experiencing a lack of power in my entire body, and I realized the efforts needed to be slow and incremental. It seemed like my body's memory of what I was able to perform was still there; the power, however,

was not. I was certain I was able to do better, so I decided to commit to the exercise schedule I had set, no matter what it took. Two things made me uneasy; the first, how my body had weakened, and the second why I was still stuck in the thought that I could still accomplish what I used to.

I had already decided that any doubt needs to be addressed at length and to understand the why. As such, no thought would be left unattended. A window opens, and unless you act on it instantaneously, it may close again. So, I either wrote down what I wanted to know more about from the ideas that came to my mind to investigate them later, or I researched the steps behind my thinking process on the spot.

Within this framework, I was able to access knowledge that I had previously ignored. I discovered the main elements I had to address; my old imprinted memories and my weakness that I thought food certainly had to do with it.

Within this fast-paced world that we live in, food has also gained in speed, as we rely heavily on fast food. We have little time to eat, and if we do eat, it is prepared speedily so we can return expeditiously to our place of work or activities. As such, we are constantly subjected to body pollutants through our food intake.

The food industry has become a world in itself

and caters to serve an ever-increasing population. This has resulted in a lower quality of food. Very few of us have time to prepare our own meals. As such, the majority of the population eats heavily processed pre-packaged foods.

Today, the food industry intentionally or unintentionally hooks its consumers on addictions to food such as sugar. The majority of the food today is produced by 10-15 big food conglomerates that control around 80% of the industry. As such, whatever those companies choose to insert in their production chain, ultimately gets transferred into our body. Sugar is a highly addictive chemical, and some studies suggest that it is more addictive than cocaine. However, it is often added to approximately all food products to enhance flavor and build the addiction.

Sugar produce is added to almost everything that we eat. Currently, it is being used across the world, irrespective of whether we should find it in these products or not. The devastating effects of sugar are very well documented. It is often considered the root source of most diseases.

Sugar is the primary nutrient for all kinds of parasites and bacteria in the body. One cannot conceive of its dangers unless one tracks its initiative process. Parasites can be introduced to the body by any means, including raw food, contaminated food, or water. Once they enter the body, they thrive on sucking energy from the body, and thus weakening it, along with its immune system.

What is most frightening about these parasites is that they proliferate mostly on sugar. The sugar cravings you can have, are the results of these parasites instructing your brain to consume more of the same product. These are intelligent creatures that construct an entire process by which they control our brain through different chemicals they secrete in the body, and electrical signals that they then relay to our brains. The signals trigger different kinds of cravings related to the food preferences we eat and can also alter one's behavior on many other levels, depending on the mode of transmission of the parasites and their origin. These are one of the many patterns. Some people often find themselves craving certain foods or behaving in a certain way due to a specific type of parasitic presence in the body.

The constant need for a particular type of food can indicate a parasitic infection in the body. For instance, being infected with a parasite while eating raw fish can result in flukes. These push the consumer to crave fish or raw fish regularly.

The food given to us in restaurants is mainly contaminated food if it is not adequately cooked or mishandled during storage. We must refrain from eating foods where we cannot trace back its source and composition and the way it has been prepared.

Most of our food consumption today consists of bad poisonous habits. Our body was never created to run on more than 99% of the food we are currently eating. We binge on sweets, junk food, and processed foods because that is what is readily available to us or what we have become accustomed to. Contemporary food is not compatible with our bodies' needs, and that negatively impacts even our smallest cell.

The lousy quality of the food we consume causes distress to our bodies and can even alter our actions.

This current consumption problem can be likened to buying a car that runs on fuel, but we are trying to feed it diesel.

We have become a blind consumable nation directed by programming, advertisement, and laziness even in our food choices. This is creating a weakness in our bodies and blurriness in our minds. Thus, it goes without saying that one could not see the beauty in life when caught up in a toxic body's gloominess, unable to perform as one should, and feeling constantly weak.

When we do realize that our energy level is low, we begin to hide behind the excuse of being tired, which is the main reason for procrastination. We keep postponing actions and duties because of our food quality and the lack of nutrients therein.

Even the food we believe is healthy and nutritional value in our diet is genetically altered and re-engineered for mass production. Moreover, we are fed chemicals of all sorts, pesticides, and hormones in large quantities, and all these are harmful for our body, organs, cells, and general well-being. If we think about what we are eating as snacks and meals, we will arrive at the sad conclusion that we have drastically altered what is present in nature and what we are indeed supposed to consume and derive our energy from, and thus, we are transforming ourselves into less effective humans.

We have grown accustomed to many unnatural products filled with sugars and carbohydrates and developed an addiction to them and use them as our fuel.

Generally speaking, the food that we ingest alters the flow of electricity in us by increasing or decreasing the acidity levels in our bodies, depending on how nutritious, fresh, and clean or otherwise, how contaminated, inadequate, and modified or polluted it is. Any imbalance increasing the acidity levels leads to a long list of diseases.

Diseases are thus a result of many factors

combined that add up to create a toxic environment within our bodies, and the fact that one is not feeling well and suffering from specific symptoms is the mere result of such imbalance. Once the balance is restored in our body, the illness will subside.

The body should run on a certain PH balance in order to operate at optimum levels. Our contemporary food intake serves to destabilize this imbalance, rendering it too difficult for any organ to function properly.

Negative thoughts can also directly result from such a PH imbalance, as an acid milieu triggers all organs, including the brain, into survival mode, and tempers with the hormone secretions. This serves to redirect our attention.

Moreover, illegal and legal drug intake has increased dramatically over the years. It is globally estimated that half a billion people use illicit drugs as per studies, ranging from cannabis to opioids. These are rough estimates, I researched on google, and I believe the numbers could be higher, which is alarming.

Whether prescribed or non-prescribed, there is an alarming number of people trying to deal with personal health unease and restlessness in their bodies and minds across the globe.

If we also take into account all people who use drugs for pleasure or those who use drugs as medicine, the numbers would be staggering. In effect, we could notice that we are a population living on toxic chemicals.

All medicines have a range of side effects, while their primary degree of success mainly depends on the placebo effect. The placebo effect is the healing mechanism the body naturally initiates when taking any pill, irrespective of its composition. Even drugs made of starch could heal us by just believing that we are taking medicine alone.

A significant part of the medicine we are consuming is useless because, in most cases, it is not the medication that heals, rather the psychological comfort of taking it. Our body and mainly our mind are very effective at healing diseases. Thus, we should try as much as possible to reduce the drug intake to avoid the side-effects of pills. In effect, we are mostly poisoning our bodies more for no reason, at a time when healing is within our reach in more natural and direct ways.

Much of the elements we take in are unsuitable for our bodies. They create all kinds of inflammations that stress our immune system and leave it in constant shock, where the body doesn't know where to start healing first.

Thus, our food intake, which contains a large spectrum of harmful bacteria and parasites that reproduce in the body and chemicals such as medicines that destabilize the good bacteria levels in us, are all leading to body poisoning and addictions. They either release addictive toxins in our system or allow flourishment of harmful organisms that affect our general health and wellbeing.

This can lead to a significant shift in our regulatory behavior and thinking process, as the memory on the cellular level relinquishes control to this imbalance and to parasites, and often, their level of reproduction is so swift that it can become a life-threatening problem.

The systematic invasion of the entire body, including the brain, weakens the immune system further. The parasites then bind to organs and cells and communicate their genetic codes to the cells, and thus the organs proliferate and continue feeding on us.

Paying attention to whatever goes into our body is not something to be taken lightly. We should treat it with respect, care, and total commitment in choosing what to eat and where to eat it, what chemicals we allow in, or what not to.

We need to protect our vessel that permits us to live these experiences.

One should keep in mind that whatever he lets in becomes Him. If we ingest an apple or drink water or coffee, it gets turned into "our body." Therefore, we must pay less attention to the marketing aspect of all products and pay more attention to the quality of what we generally consume, being of whatever nature.

TWO

MIND POLLUTION

OUR BRAIN IS an essential part of our body. It is the ultimate organizer and reader of all internal organs and the principal organ that keeps all internal operations working correctly. The brain relies mainly on food to keep up with the daily internal activities in the body and our everyday functions. Thus, having a healthy body is a critical factor in having a more relaxed, powerful, and practical mind.

All the creativity in this world and all that will ever happen; all inventions, productions, and innovations, are a direct result of our minds set in motion. The power of our mind is unlimited and beyond imagination.

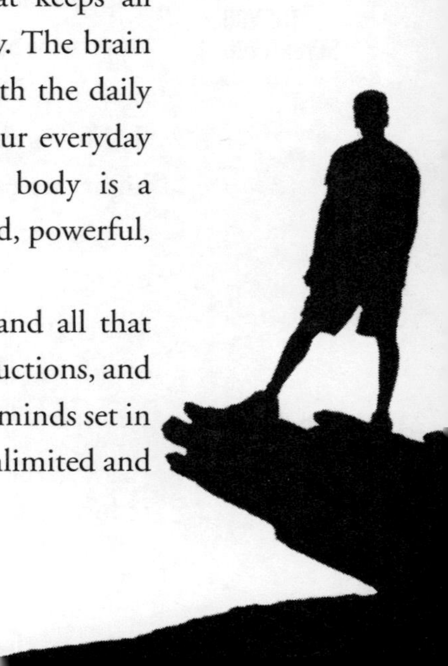

What 'currently exists' and what has taken place in our reality so far results from our collective desires, thoughts, and actions accumulated throughout history. Desire, which in general is an unconscious state of mind, acts as the primary generator of thoughts and actions that motivate our reality. Desire is the process through which what does not exist thrives to become real and parallels our efforts. Thus, what exists cannot become what it is without thought and action. As such, what exists and what does not exist, combined, are essential components that define existence as we extract all that can exist from what does not exist.

Humanity can impact what exists, but they know not how to realize what does not. The importance of our human mind, which is responsible for our thoughts, is that it is the only way by which we can turn what does not exist into the first stage of its existence. The more fruitful and goal-oriented our thoughts are, the higher we can advance in the realm of our reality.

As a result of our thoughts, actions constitute energy, and the more actions we are willing to take, the more torque this adds to this circle of life. Collective consciousness is like in the example of an electric circuit where we increase the voltage by adding more electrons to it or reduce it to null by removing electrons. Actions need sustainability to keep the flow ongoing even at the minor individual level.

We are all formed of the same genes, an approximate number of cells; thus, we are all identical in nature. However, people's thoughts and actions differ across humanity. Some lean more towards thoughts while others rely entirely on actions, while some others depend on both.

Personality disorders and emotional complexes are on the rise, as we are misusing the power of desire, thought, and action hierarchy. We are dimming the light on conscious desire and limiting our thinking process. As a result, actions are becoming more chaotic as they are driven by pure impulsiveness. Thoughts that serve to regulate and filter desires are becoming products that are cast on the shelf, with our actions now reflecting our lack of desire or spontaneity.

The problem is that most of us are made to think horizontally through little planning. We are driven to limit ourselves to our surroundings and are thus unable to operate at optimum levels. We have been transformed into a society of mass consumers of all kinds, including thoughts.

The problem is that whether this is intentional or not, it is imposed on our current way of life.

The ability to properly operate in life and reach where we aim to reach relies purely on the mind, not only on the mind but rather on the purity of our mind. The mind has two sides to maintain, the biological and the thought process. We will elaborate on the latter, in this chapter.

Mental health and the reorganization of our thoughts and desires in the action pyramid are essential for our fruitful advancement towards expansion rather than regression.

Today, however, the rise in the number of borderline personalities, from narcissists to sociopaths and many other types of mental illnesses, is due to this lack of organization. These illnesses are either rooted biologically or are mental disorders related to how the mind is conditioned. Mental disorders have several categories: biological or psychological, such as congenital disabilities, DNA defects, and trauma to the brain. However, in most cases, they are due to negative mind habituation. Thus, most of these disorders result from our compounded experiences, our thinking mode, and our unconscious negative behaviors. The leading cause of the increase of mental disorders in our present-day is exposure to many types of pollutants that affect biology and psychology.

Life is becoming increasingly fast and requires more concentration to be able to maneuver. However, our level of focus is decreasing due to the amount of information our brain is constantly bombarded with. People spend more time on televisions, and social media, unaware of the danger of having this information stored in the subconscious mind. Subliminal messages, intended for marketing, and harmful material from all over, destructively impact the brain, triggering it to manufacture a virtual world and dimension to our existence.

Our subconscious mind that acts as a recorder does not differentiate between what is real and what is not real and thus keeps playing unconscious ideas on repeat in our minds. This living model serves to create a life of unease where the line between the real and imaginary is blurred.

This autopilot mode we have switched our minds to has created a new social order: the definition of chaos both on a social and internal level.

Thus, what is not real is slowly but consistently becoming our reality, as we have allowed our subconscious to dictate what we should or should not believe. The mental process by which we have built a complex network linked by electric waves has become erratic as the electricity within is channeled in chaos.

We have been programmed to a separate frequency, other than the one we were initially created to experience. Thus, the state of our existing world is far removed from what it should be.

Whether this new scenario and mind programming is set by some large corporations that control almost all media, from TV channels to social media, is yet to be determined. Regardless, the fact remains that we are being directed towards a path filled with negativity, and mind control.

The media plays the role of steel bars that act to maintain humanity within set boundaries, serving to reduce our mental abilities to the resolution of menial tasks. We are induced into feelings of personal anguish and torment, and unless we become aware of our existing reality and its negative impact on our lives, we will remain conditioned to our current state of being. Many of us return home at the end of the day, unaware of the source of our unease. We lay on our couches and watch TV serving only to exacerbate the problem. Being conditioned by our environment is very detrimental to our state of being and threatens the core of our existence. It entails ultimate passivity, and unconsciously triggers mental imbalances.

What's more, this modern state of being is acting to limit our brain capacity beneath its true potential, to an extent where we become mentally crippled while living under the illusion that we are gaining more knowledge from these information sources that are limiting us.

Mind pollution is distracting us from our true life purpose. It has resulted in people always seeking to alter their realities to achieve meaning by hiding behind social media profiles and acting from behind masks. This, in turn, results in more social dissonance and superficial relationships based on appearances.

Negative mind programming is currently taking over the globe, through news blitzed from all directions, imprinting all the negativity into our state of being. Watching a horror movie for the first time can have a significant psychological and tormenting effect on anyone watching. After being watched multiple times, the shock effect is somewhat mitigated. We are numbed on the outside while believing it does not affect us from within, but the truth is that it does. It disturbs us on all levels through our subconscious minds without fail. That is how programming works. Whatever we experience becomes engraved as data in our memory while we are completely unaware of it.

Whenever we let our brain get accustomed to negativity, our approach to life goes down a poisonous wormhole.

Our mode of thinking is being polluted by so many programs that our subconscious records in an alarming way.

When we are watching the television, we

realize that most programs are flooded with violent graphic scenes in films and on the news that invade our subconscious and become its sustenance. When we encounter negativity and bad experiences in our real life, we relate it to the information already stored in our minds and subconsciously deal with them with our imprinted thoughts. We engage without thinking about the consequences. We thus transform into negative, harmful beings, spreading negativity into our immediate surroundings without even realizing it.

People who can kill, get accustomed to such acts. Most criminals do not show remorse and are unaffected by their actions. Soldiers are similarly programmed to act without too much questioning, although much sorrow can ensue such actions. What begins small, grows with time. This is the law of existence. To add more to what is already available and what is already existent. What 'is there' will attract more of its exact nature. Life is a big game of constant accumulation.

So even being subjected to the smallest concealed negative externality is awfully impactful.

Since the day we were born, we begin taking on negative behavior patterns and add yet more negativity to them.

That can be noticed by watching today's moral degrading standards. Morality is shifting and, in a way, is being degraded, as we become more harmful to others and our surroundings with every coming generation. What was considered a taboo before, is now fully acceptable.

That is dismembering the very foundation of our societies and creating an environment of uneasiness in our lives.

Was this intentionally created to keep people at bay from the fear of the unknown? What is evident is that the human brain is undoubtedly being subjected to many shocks every day from everywhere. We are living a full-fledged "Alice in Wonderland" syndrome. News and negativity keep us bound to "wrongs" by keeping us under the influence of the "Stockholm Syndrome". Our reality is being manipulated from what it actually is, to a reality the media wants us to see.

Fear, negativity, and abnormal social manners are presented to us daily to the extent that it becomes habitual and ordinary. We thus are currently experiencing our reality through completely unreal life experiences. On the unconscious level, things are confused, with no set of directions, where we always try to seek any outlet to escape it, which is confusing based on the desperation this carries.

People seem to have invested so much into

their misery on physical and psychological levels to an extent, that they feel they cannot return to the point of equilibrium, no matter how many times they attempt to.

Overhauling one's entire life can be a daunting task. But we can easily accomplish that once it becomes a conviction and we become aware that it is a must-do.

It just needs to be taken on, one part at a time, with consistency and resilience.

THREE

RESTORING OUR BODY AND MIND

WE HAVE BECOME a melting pot of negativity, accumulating bad habits and bad food, yet we essentially remain optimistic dreamers. We want to have it all in life, fortune, happiness, good health, and prosperity. Everyone dreams of becoming a well-established individual. Many of us believe we can, but "can" is not "is." Can is a possibility that needs to manifest itself to become concrete.

"When drowning in a sea of chaos, nothing can work in our favor."

Universal laws cannot prosper under such toxic environments. Everything in life is based on laws, and those laws in turn are based on a set of rules that demand a level of organization and respect.

One cannot have an ill body, a toxic mind, suffering both internally on the most microcell level and externally on most of their interactions and one fine day we just decide to show up and ask the Universe, in a moment of despair, for things to improve.

"Goals need to be built incrementally." For things to change, we must begin by changing our approach. From the beginning of our existence, and for the rest of our lives, we expect to achieve only happiness. But we often forget that reaching happiness requires much work on both the physical and psychological levels. Happiness demands implementing behavioral changes and maintenance habits that can enrich us, and allow a life of positivity to flourish.

"To change, one must imagine himself reborn the moment he decides to alter his life." As such, we need to treat ourselves with as much compassion as possible, and be merciful to ourselves to achieve success.

To create a constructive environment for happiness, we must walk the extra mile with dedicated life goals. Remember, we are trying to tread on the other side to achieve ultimate joy, and we must leave all old 'negative trophies' behind, as we need to carry less weight as possible.

Before contemplating the thought of calling on laws that go beyond ourselves, like the laws of attraction, the law of cause and effect etc. We must first work on the laws that lie within. Thus, taking the what's "within" to the what's "without".

At times, people find luck and succeed in life, but if the within is left unattended, their success would be partial, and all could be lost if not properly maintained. Getting lucky is a probability that relies only on a fragile chance and does not sustain a lasting long-term effect. Although getting lucky and succeeding in a particular instance is possible, the result of a whole life that relies only on chance has more risks than rewards. While some might be born into a wealthy family, have caring parents, and have access to whatever they desire, this does not mean that they will go on to lead a life of happiness.

The general consensus in today's society is based on feelings of misery and scarcity. We have wielded a hostile world around us and intoxicated ourselves to the extent of numbness. The more fundamental question remains as to our ability to survive in such an environment.

To properly operate, we must first implement the right foundations by aligning ourselves internally, then following that externally towards our chosen objective. Once this alignment occurs, proper channels can be established, and the proper flow of energy can synchronize between the inner and outer layers of our being.

Take, for instance, a garden: in order to make it beautiful and plant roses, we must first plan out the suitable method for irrigation and make the grounds fertile. We seldom dedicate the same determination to our bodies and minds.

Detoxifying the body is lengthy, and can sometimes take years or lifetimes, as it is taken in stages. The first stage is to purify the body from all toxic foods, refined carbs, and sugars that we discussed. We begin by cutting out all refined sugars, which can be a daunting task at first. The cravings we subsequently feel are mainly due to parasites that feed on these sugars calling the substance out, as well as from the addiction our cells built over time through withdrawing energy from the substance.

When we deprive parasites or other organisms of their best food, they emit chemicals in our body that then send a message to the brain to demand the substance which is being cut-off. That could turn to be a very unpleasant feeling, very hard to overcome.

Once we remove sugar or any addictive substance from our diet, we begin to feel less active in the short-term, but a lot more energetic in the long one. Our mood will start improving with each single day, and we will feel refreshed.

We are cleaning the body of the killer organisms that we introduced for long in our bodies throughout the years. It is a daunting task that needs much patience.

At this stage, one can also consider taking anti-parasitic medication for a brief period to expedite the process and get rid of any lagging health issues.

I believe that all human diseases are directly linked to parasites, and the fact that we keep feeding these vermin and consequently create the most favorable environment for bad bacteria to proliferate creates a weakened body, where everything goes wrong from blood pressure to pulse to hormones regulation. In such an environment, our immune system cannot regulate or give cells instructions to fight intruders, and all kinds of diseases can flourish.

After cutting out the named pollutants, one could begin revising other components of their diet.

The human body was created to work on natural foods. Most of us are feeding it on processed junk food, injected with many chemicals. In short, "we run our bodies on poison throughout our life and believe that we enjoy it."

The process of decontamination requires full commitment and patience. Breaking one addiction at a time is a real but necessary struggle.

It can all be achieved with the right mindset.

Adding to this, the benefits of including vitamin C supplements and multivitamins in our diet during the cleansing period would also be beneficial. To further offer nutrients to our cells and restore the PH balance in the body when cells reach their correct performance levels. I also suggest taking a tablespoon of sodium bicarbonate in a glass of water early in the morning as it renders the body alkaline as it should be.

Other natural remedies that can also make a big difference in the healing process include turmeric, cloves, and coconut oil. Comprehensively, this approach will boost energy in the short and long term by ridding our bodies of all toxins and foreign bodies. The parasitic overgrowth is the result of our poor daily consumption and what is weird is that large pharmaceutical companies are also involved in the international arena in the production of unhealthy fast foods that trigger several illnesses. That might leave us wondering!

Ridding one's body of these toxins and acquired awareness will prevent future infections and illnesses.

We must eat healthy foods, spend more time and energy required to research all that we are eating, and lean more towards organic food. Our carbohydrate intake must be cut out or reduced to its minimum, as most carbohydrates available in the market are processed.

Nature is our best source of health. Thus reducing consumption to only natural elements would be most beneficial.

All diseases are derived from nature, and thus their cure can equally be found in nature". Consuming golden milk on a daily basis, once in the morning or once in the evening before bed, would be advised. The drink consists of turmeric, ginger, pepper and lemon boiled for a couple of minutes. Some people add honey to it and almond milk, but I prefer to add butter, olive oil and citrus to it with salt. Turmeric and ginger are medicinal plants not to be taken lightly and if you do this for a period of time, rest assured that you will never get ill again. It is a natural cure for chronic illnesses, as they both contain natural chemicals that help fight many ailments.

However, the benefits of eating right will not show most of the time immediately, as our body has grown accustomed to our previous diet to the extent that it has become embossed in our cells.

Our bodies got used for so long on vibrating at the frequencies these foods offer, upwarding the process into an obsession.

Detoxifying for complete healing is a lengthy process that will show its benefits with time.

All that is discussed above shows the strong

bond between us and what we interact with on the molecular level. The more we eat something, and interact with it by letting it become part of our reality, the more that thing becomes suitable and tolerable to us, regardless if it harms us or not.

The process also reveals an exchange of data within us and within our food intake that keeps the bond ongoing.

People, I think, select their diet and food preferences based on memory arising from their personal experience when interacting with their food and the subsequent feelings the experience generates in their bodies, and the sensory experience stemming from consuming certain nutrients.

Our eating habits are thus a direct result of different memories at play. It is an array of taste, smell, and sensory memories combined.

All this demonstrates that food is a personal "free" choice and a conditional choice based on an entire memory interface between us and food. The link between our diverse memories, which are contained in a multitude of our cells, and those that exist in the food we consume at this stage becomes clearer. It is an acquired link between the memory that runs in our bodies through our brain and senses and the memory that runs in food, in its texture, smell and taste.

Since this is acquired and built on the memory

level over a long time, switching to healthy foods requires a regimented effort to erase old acquired memories and build new ones.

We must proceed to delete all memories previously assembled and begin stamping new food experiences as new memories on our mental and biological levels. This, I believe, is the best way we would be able to overcome addictions.

Once we can put our bodies on the right track to restore our body balance on a cellular and biological level, the second phase of purification, which is cleansing our minds of pollutants, can be undertaken, as it becomes clearer to us how to do it and less painful. For mind detoxification to succeed, more significant efforts are required as it is a game of will and persistence. Removing elements of mind toxicity, given how our minds are programmed, is no easy task; it is a tabula rasa process.

We have developed over the years powerful addictions that have acted to destroy our ability to prosper and create the life of abundance we so long for. To dismantle all this, we need a very dedicated process that requires devotion, patience, conviction, and a lot of stubbornness. The process begins by filtering all the thoughts that we have allowed to enter our minds. Imagine a physical screen inside your mind that determines the thoughts we let in and those we do not. Thus, we should become more conscious of our thoughts and accord ourselves the proper time needed to think about what we think of. Once we master the awareness of what we are thinking, we can begin reflecting on our ideas and whether they are worthy of becoming a part of us or not. This is the first step to control the subconscious mind, as we are determining now what we attribute more importance to and what we let become a part of our mind.

If the ideas or thoughts that come to your mind are negative, you can develop techniques to remove them before they are born, never letting them enter the unconscious sphere. The methods are all yours to invent, but you must rely on your awareness that you should remove negative thoughts at all costs, as soon as they come to your mind, by disregarding them and replacing them with other more pleasant scenarios. That will also automatically allow for more positive thinking due to the absence of negativity and lead to a healthier thinking process.

Some negative thoughts are so powerful that we cannot forget them easily. Those should be set aside and ignored during the day to logically deal with them when time allows to sort matters out calmly. Thus, no negative thought should be kept unattended and full attention to untie your life should be accorded. Whilst small negative, irrelevant thoughts can be directly shut down in your head, bigger issues need a lot of thinking about how to dissolve them. They, however, should not become a worrying obsession, as what emerges always subsides, and when you are calm and think logically, all can be resolved.

In the example of a thought that keeps coming to mind, it will be an arduous process of determining where we must try again until the thought dissipates. The persistence of some ideas not to leave our minds is mainly due to the fear factor arising of the outcomes of what those thoughts could represent in our future if they materialize.

Fear is not real, and believe me when I say that it is today's most dangerous mental illness our civilization is facing. Our fears are all the result of this mass hallucination driven to us by the negativity from the media or the result of a lack of knowledge to deal with, a certain matter or an event.

Most of what we fear does not happen, and if we educate ourselves and get the proper knowledge to resolve the situations we fear, fear subsides. Unless one keeps fearing outcomes irrationally and remains ignorant or blind to how to solve matters, one will never invite unpleasant scenarios to happen in life.

Be bold when dealing with your fears and

negative thoughts and show full control and believe it or not, the majority will dissipate.

At this stage, some people in our lives will dislike our new reality when they notice a change for the better. But do not let that discourage you. Others will disappear from your life under the excuse that they do not recognize you anymore. Some at this stage you will let go as you also must begin to filter out some people in your entourage that constitute a negative influence on your well-being.

"This might be painful, but it is necessary."

Many just give up and stop trying at this stage, as they let desperation take over and go through life just expressing how unfair and discriminating it is and how people are judgmental and harsh at times.

Well, I have never seen anything fairer than life. What you invest in and let in prospers and multiplies.

Consider your life as an equation of a+b+c. When the equation is such, you always get back as results combinations of the givens you already set and incorporated in your way of living on different levels before, like aa+b+ccc or a+bbb+ccc.

When working on your equation of a+b+c, make sure that all givens are positive and meaningful. At times people might get in your life and drop in a (d).

For example, you are working on a specific project, and someone criticizes you and starts to downplay your efforts. This criticism might agitate you in a way. You might begin to shout at that person out of irritation about what he/she said or did. This occurrence has now added to your life a new given which is harmful. This new (d) has rendered your life's equation as an a+b+c+d. Although what you incorporated up to this point were all positive. A new negative variable was added without even you realizing it.

One might argue that this was just a small irrelevant reaction, and I did not start it. It does not count in the 'who I am, what I want in life' equation.

Reactions are actions, and everything counts, even the smallest of things.

We take our negative reactions to others as an excuse to continue doing wrong while entitling it with natural behavior and response. It is not. You have incorporated the reaction in the equation, no matter what the trigger was, so it counts. If you are getting bad results, it is mostly because of all the culmination of your previous unconscious "d"s thoughts and actions that you allowed in.

So, check what you are adding as variables objectively and screen your (d)s. Cut off anyone or anything that activates your (d)s or just simply change your reaction or find adequate solutions.

Even the smallest negative action or thought that you believe does not matter really matters to a very great extent as it all adds up with time. Accept the bad occurrences and move on. Try your best to look at the bigger picture, regardless of how many push backs you face. You have a lot of power in you, more than you can ever imagine. It would help if you refuse to live a limited life and be proactive. It is difficult to initially implement this way of thinking as it was never part of the unconscious program you have built for yourself in the past and is a new way to deal with things, but this is for your best interest. One should ultimately reach the conviction that he is an unstoppable being driven by the good energy because he is. In so doing, the only true friend you can have at this point is you. No one else is capable of aiding you in your efforts. It is a singular path one must take alone.

In some instances, this journey can become daunting but do not let despair take over. Life is ever fair as you can reap whatever you sow. Stop being angered by the actions of others because you would be incorporating the anger factor into your life.

Stop finding excuses and get to work on yourself. If others make you angry, think more rationally and cut conversations short if they are unproductive. Do not get outraged at anything, especially problems that people project on you. People always tend to argue that they are right at showing aggression to others under so many excuses to alleviate culpability. These types of behavior are not correct and should be stopped. The actions of others should not impact how we choose to treat others. We build our internal programs by repetition within all aspects, from food to thoughts and actions. So, start on your new program.

The more you act consciously and in repetition, the more it becomes you. Breaking programmed associations can be difficult as we consider them against our will since we originally approved them into our system. However, what is wrong is wrong, no matter the pleasure it creates in the short run. One should always keep in mind a set of positive ideas that have special meaning and use them to fight the negative ideas that automatically pop into our mind.

Humans process through their brains between 50,000 to 60,000 thoughts on an average per day. Most of them are negative, I believe. Consciously watch what you think of during a single day and see the proof for this. So, you can imagine how much negativity you are subjecting your brain to, every day. Multiply that by 365 days, and you can get an idea of how much negative thoughts enter your mind every year. Filtering with repetition will slowly become an innate reaction, and you will be screening negative ideas and letting them out, and letting in positive thoughts and ideas unconsciously as life unfolds. Stop blaming your failures on the outside world. To blame-shift failure from our side on everything around us is a weakness we should mitigate. Nothing that happens to us internally is the product of what happens on the external level, unless we allow it to become so. Once you take control of your life, your conscious comportment can ultimately change the outside world you live in. When negative things happen, you must learn how to filter them, and deal with the situation objectively while remaining detached. That would enhance your thinking mechanism, and give you power over any situation, including your weaknesses.

The second step would be to remove all other external sources of negativity. This would include television, social media, and all other media that relay negative images, and ideas to your mind without you being able to control its impact. If you do not realize and become aware of how to use these tools in a 'conscious positive manner' in your life, never attend to these again.

When you are done with the process of clearing all body, and mind pollutants from your life, you are back into operational mode, and then around 50 trillion cells in your body can work properly once again—your power, whether mental or physical, will be restored. What is most important about this process is not only that you will become healthier, but that you will now be able to direct the energy towards whatever goal you desire productively. Your 50 trillion cells generate an average of 0.7 volts per cell. You can now fully grasp how much power is running through your body and mind. You can also discover your abilities to redirect such energies into more productive tasks. You can now start using your body to emit and absorb energy from and to the outside.

You are an electric being, run entirely by electricity, and this electricity generates the magnetism and the frequencies required to lead healthy lives, the way you intended to live, and attract whatever you want to draw from the outside.

We and all beings and all elements in this universe are interconnected through energy, magnetism, and frequencies produced by electricity.

You have a conscious job to undertake to recognize what is detoxifying your body in order to operate properly in this matrix.

The body is a complex machine, and if you do not organize it properly, it will take you on a negative journey and a crazy rollercoaster, both physically and psychologically.

To go beyond complexity, the simplest assumption is to make sure you let in only good quality consumables, at all levels.

We should reach the conviction that if we do not get our mind programmed ourselves, our minds will get programmed through external and internal means. And if we do not shape our body, it will get shaped by its desires. Moreover, we should remove all fears from our daily lives as the majority of what we have feared throughout our lives are paper giants like we have discussed.

We have based so much of our life on conditioning, and the belief that we believe whatever we are told to be true must be true is actually invalid. Moreover, we should work on what we present to those around us and pay close attention to what others offer to us. Lying, plotting, conspiring, and trying to deal with others in an unethical manner; all these will derail you from the main path you have set for yourself, and will lead you where you do not wish to go. The truth always finds its way. So, you must be vigilant not to offer them to anyone and not to let anyone introduce them in your life.

Furthermore, all this will create negative scenarios down the road. Usually, lies need a lot to be maintained, and are so averse and can lead one to become pathologically sick.

Our inner voice usually tells us what is

wrong in our lives, from food to many other wrong choices we make. However, there is always something that makes us lean towards shutting this voice up and continuing with the addictions we have accumulated. We must always listen to this hunch and never go against it, as it is our body and mind telling us we are going in the wrong direction. We have been addicted to short doses of high adrenaline in whatever we do, and away from the simpler life, we are meant to lead. This new path requires all our senses, thoughts, and conscious mind to be lined up towards our general well-being.

When this happens on the inside, all environmental stimuli or experiences will have no internal effect on us. The harmful elements will get automatically filtered by the system we have put in place. Moreover, one should give great importance to breathing, as it is the entire body's regulator and the main source of life. Try not to breathe for a few minutes and see what happens. We rarely breathe consciously and think very little of this process, which is crucial to maintaining a good life. Once the body and mind are cleansed of toxins, the first breaths are usually doubled. That is because the body needs oxygen to compensate for the toxin suffocation we had been subjecting it to. When fully detoxified with time, you would notice breathing is deeper, but less often. This is the sign that you have found your balance.

At this level, you are working on changing your body and mind and programming them into more effective choices that will improve the quality of your life, health, and the control you have, over your future. This works because you are imprinting your body and mind with new memory particles, and deleting your program's old memory. A more profound phenomenon is now taking place. You are creating a new you.

Currently, we are living in an era ruled by image consultants, where the majority of what we see outside is fake. From actors to famous people to politicians, to bloggers, they all are letting us see another shining image of the world, however, the inside is shallow and empty. Real change is not about shining your outside image so you can get more followers on Instagram or more votes in the elections, but it is instead a job, intended first for your mental and physical health before anything else, to be complete on the inside. Once you have cleaned what is inside, the image you project will directly reflect this change and shine by itself. The process is achieved by you, towards a less chaotic state of being. Upon completing the restoration of your body and mind, you can begin by adding up the necessary steps to flourish on all levels.

FOUR

GETTING IMPRINTED WITH THE CORRECT MEMORY

WHILE WORKING ON clearing many pollutants of the body and mind, things become more evident, and a guaranteed deep feeling of wellness prevails. At this level, one starts wondering how this same being with the same cells, organs, and brain, shifted his own life, which he always viewed in one direction, to a broader, more explicit dimension. The process of change itself is so meaningful as it requires moving from one level to another. This change happens by imprinting our biological body with new memories different from the ones that were already there.

When we exercise, the pressure and vibrations produced are stored in our muscles as memory,

which is later reflected in muscles' size and shape. The brain carries out the process of storing the movements. Every day the brain stores new thoughts and actions through electrical imprinting, which on revisiting becomes refined ideas and necessary information.

All atoms, cells, and organs in our bodies have different abilities to store memory in them and not only our brain. And I believe the motto that "we are what we think," which we have been taught throughout our history, is not too accurate. We are rather all that our body stores as memory and should treat our thinking process in that context, with the thinking being the ability to read this data in a simple or complex manner.

Thoughts are generated by all parts of our body and processed in the brain, which is only one part of our thinking mechanism and plays the role of a memory reader. Muscles, bones, and all organs store different types of memories and also play a major role in the thinking process as they share all their memory with the brain to take note of it and use it as and when needed. Our brain cannot work as-is unless connected through electricity to all our cells. The brain exchanges information, back and forth, transferring it to the destined cells making sure the sensed information is stored and shared with the destined cell.

Come to think of it, if during exercising,

the information was not stored in the muscles, then instead of bulging muscles, we would have a voluminous brain. What happens during this exercise is that pressure builds new memory in our muscles where it is stored. Our brain, in return, gets information of this stored memory in our cells and registers the occurrence. Thus, in this example, memory is stored in the muscles and brain.

If we give the whole mechanism that runs our lives a close look and scrutinizes and analyze the processes involved, one will discover that all that makes our life possible the way it is, is mainly memory imprinting, i.e., the ability to acquire new information from other types of memories. Let us interpret this from our inside out.

Imagine we wake up one day having lost all memory related to what happened in our life or in our world and not a single memory of who we are. What would that feel like? One can try to imagine himself in that situation for a while. We would not even notice that we can even start remembering what we know, as we will not even remember that we know anything. Even if we keep the rest of our life thinking and scratching our brain, we will never be able to reach anywhere with a memory and information-depleted brain. Existence will have no meaning, and we would not even know that we exist as we will have no memory of anything that exists.

Our existence's mere reality lies in our body having memory storage abilities that can be modified by accumulation, and this storage is the constituent of everything within, in different forms, shapes, and with different roles and is modeled and directed unconsciously or consciously on several levels. That is what creates the ability to wake up every day and continue from where we left the previous day, as all is stored from the first atom to the whole of the body.

Now imagine on another level that one day our cells and organs lose the data and memory stored in them, and so did the atoms contained therein, both on the genetic memory level or the sensory memory level. Even if we try to recall on the conscious and unconscious levels, our bodies will immediately collapse, causing chaos within, and life would not be anything like we generally can experience. We can vanish on the spot. Therefore, this embossing process on the atoms and cells level with genetic memory mainly, which is unconscious and other sensory memories on top, which are conscious, is essential for our existence and these atoms being part of a bigger mechanism which is the molecules, have two levels of memory exchange, one on the level of the atom and the second on the molecular level. This hierarchy goes on as such in the body at all levels. This storage and imprinting process is the motor of life across the Universe, as it allows the storage and exchange of all information between everything that exists. The exchange of memory throughout our bodies can take many forms depending on the experiences, knowledge, events, skills, or repetition. It varies from genetic to sensory, implicit, explicit, declarative, procedural, episodic, semantic, and inwards and outwards imprinting.

But these are partial definitions of what memory is, as memory cannot be divided into categories as it remains, in essence, the same is with different data. What can be segregated, though, is the information stored within. Memory storage we will refer to as particles, as they are tiny unseen particles that go senseless to us, are like a sponge and mirror simultaneously, and are physical rather than abstract. Thus, they exchange information by binding to each other on all existence levels. Our muscles, for instance, store "procedural" information when we exercise. The more exercises we do, the more we increase the information in "basic" memory. It, in turn, generates different categories of memories, which are extracted from this "procedural" memory.

Thus, the particles in our muscle suck the particles in the vibration from exercise, and keep it in the muscle, where it becomes a part of it by binding to it.

Information needs storage, and a place to be saved. The storage is everywhere as these particles constitute everything, and are information magnets and reservoirs. They gather to form additional storage and disperse to join other particles based on vibrations they are subjected to in the body. However, they are also present in preset packages like atoms, which are organized programming memory particles, set at higher levels of existence than ours. Several types of frequencies and vibrations can lead to two or more particles binding and start imprinting each other. The gained information is either summed up on top of available information or achieves domination over total imprinting of the other, overriding other memory information depending on the level of vibration. Thus, at the source of existence, settles at our level of existence cannot be overridden with any existing strong memory, as the first imprinting is much vigorous than the acquired one. Genetic memory is imprinted on top of existing memory in particles, which can also be imprinted on top of any information we desire.

Let us take the physical exercise we have done before. Memory arising from the vibration due to pressure was added to the existing genetic memory already in the cell, which determines the atoms of muscle, cell shape, and quantity which are all in turn imprinted on memory from the source that constitutes the storage particles. The genetic memory was imprinted by accumulating sensory memory on top, thus staying as a genetic memory and accumulating other weaker memories only being sensory. Full overriding can only occur either at the same level of imprinting only, i.e., genetic can override genetic, sensory can override sensory or a higher memory overriding a lower, such genetic overriding sensory.

Therefore, when we were earlier reducing the toxicity in our body and mind and filtering negativity, we unconsciously initiated the process of imprinting a better person's memories. While shifting to better ideas, judgments, foods, and body fuel, we overrode the person we were by adding new memories on top of all existing memories and overriding some. As one can realize at a later stage, this process of imprinting is planting new seeds on a very fertile ground. The seeds we now plant grow into, abundant crop as it is of better quality than the ones we used to plant before. We are all sowers and reapers without even realizing it. This actuality is always accurate that we always reap what we sow. If one analyzes his life objectively at any moment, he could easily realize that, what is at present, is a direct result of what he previously planted and worked on accumulating. Like muscles that gain new memory by exercising, our thoughts, and consequently, our actions, hold the seeds for our future. Sooner or later, we see them multiply, defining our life.

This mental imprinting can take place in all our bodies to different extents, from the smallest atom to the biggest thought we may have. When we were eating better quality food, particles in this food turned into us. Thus, we end up having better quality cells formed out of better particles. The same goes for our minds when we store new and more positive, fruitful ideas. So, we fully run on whatever information in any type of particles we let in on different levels in our life throughout our existence. When we eat a certain food, we do not just acquire nutrients. We also acquire atoms and the information contained therein.

The information-holding atoms make all the difference in the kinds of food we consume and how it affects us. An avocado, for instance, decomposes into smaller nutrients such as fat, proteins, and carbohydrates when eaten. These nutrients, in turn, further decompose into vitamins and amino acids. It further decomposes to the level required by our body and absorbed by our body until it reaches the basic pure memory particles level that we are not aware of. The imprinting of the apple we ate stays until these particles join other memory particles in our body. These particles exchange information that is already available in our body's genetic memories, and the banana being the weaker memory between it and our body becomes us.

Moreover, when we watch a movie or hear the news, memory particles are carried over to us through light or sound waves and stored in our bodies' adequate parts. These memory particles are transported by electricity, a medium for our eyes, to the brain from where it is sent to the right storage place, where it becomes part of us. Apart from that, it could be stored in our brain and other parts in other areas of our body depending on the information these particles carry.

Pain by being hit by a rock, for instance, is being imprinted on us through vibration consisting of particles, on our skin or muscle or bone, where these particles get through the skin/bone/muscle, etc. turned into electricity by receptors on our skin, and travel directly to the brain, through the adequate channels being the neurons, where it is read and stored. Based on the memories of such incidents stored in it, the brain sends signals composed of memory particles carrying the information required to be acted upon to the concerned parts of our body. It also sends signals to our skin if the vibrations were strong enough to act in a specific way.

Having an objective reflection on whatever

we have worked on gathering throughout these years from everywhere in this context is a must. At this current moment, both our body and mind are the image and sum of all conscious and subconscious information in memory particles we have gathered and stored in before.

Whether this information is related to genetics acquired from our parents or consumed food and acquired experiences, it is all memory and is stored in us in memory particles. Apart from that, imprinting can also occur through information-filled floating memory particles available around us. When stored in us, all information is reflected on our inside and outside. They shape our interiors, including our thinking process, and therefore determine our general well-being and actions that control our exterior. The information gathered can be shared with our inside as well as our outside with any kind of element we choose in unlimited potentials through our conscious or unconscious state and actions related thereto. There is unlimited potential as to how we can model ourselves and our environments given that accumulation. The memory we gather can be extracted from everything around us and how we experience it at all levels, and it is the direct result of all that we see, experience, feel, taste, smell, or hear. Our atoms are made from trillions of memory particles that we cannot sense or see, and that are continuously being imprinted by exposure to everything seen or unseen.

When the imprinting of newly acquired information happens on top of existing prior memories like atoms, cells, organs, or our whole body and further accumulation occurs, the larger the memory association becomes, higher the directed purpose would be. In our bodies, the organ memory and role prevails over the role of the cells, so do the cells over the molecules and molecules over atoms. When a cell is isolated, the memory particles within it shift their purpose to cater to the cell function, unlike when it was part of the organ. Still, when the cell is a part of an organ, the particles within are to maintain the cell working correctly but are directed to a larger extent to serve the bigger association purpose, which is the organ. That is because vibrations at the higher levels keep all that is below vibration-wise aligned.

The power of pure memory available in us and our environment is that it can be turned back and forth to and from frequency to send it across the same channels we receive it by. It is sent in the form of vibrations, frequencies, and electricity. It could happen horizontally in our social environment through different means and mechanisms in our brain; one of them is thought. One materialization of this is speaking, which is a vertical emission of this memory to imprint other memories on the same level. The more we understand this memory concept, which forms us and everything around us on the whole existence level, the more proper channels we can build. These channels then transfer more information between the entire Universe and us, depending on the signal's strength. The better the signal, the better our outside imprinting will be. At a certain level of consciousness, one can easily detract more quality free particle memory from his environment and use it for his good.

The environment is not referred to as only nature. Nature is a big part of our environment. At our existence level, it refers to everything, including the unseen, which is often regarded as emptiness and nothingness. Emptiness is material, and it exists in a form we cannot sense and is filled with the purest forms of memory particles of higher imprinting from "The Source," which we cannot read but which is connected to everything in what we can sense. This channeling and feeling connected to everything we refer to as faith, love, and empathy are all physical and are the direct exchange of particles between the various recipients, entities, objects, beings, and us. The purer this connection is, and the more frequently we stay aware and conscious of it, the more the possibilities will be, to access even higher memories with higher imprinting at different existence levels and attract them to us to alter our internal memory through external memory in ways we never thought would be possible. Thus, allowing us to elevate our energy and be in harmony within.

The more relevant the memory we store, the more memory from this memory can be generated, and the more knowledge we could gain by building on this relevancy. This also goes for any material or element that exists in this world to lower or higher extents. This depends on how much memory ability these entities can use to store, model, or generate. What gives us humans an edge on everything else, including other living animals, is our ability to accumulate memory in more considerable quantities and the more advanced reader of this memory we possess.

Repetition over a considerable time, commitment, action, and devotion are all ways of imprinting that allow us to increase the effectiveness of what we store as information and how we can use it through action. Multitudes of research have been conducted on the ability of elements to store memory.

However, we will take the example of water, even though every element is equipped with such abilities based on memory exchange. Water, for instance, despite being a simple element made of hydrogen and oxygen, can store memory in so many forms. Many experiments conducted on it confirmed beyond doubt that it could store different kinds of memory.

This is imprinting in its most concrete form. It is shown beyond doubt through experiments that water can even store feelings. A lot of scientists like Dr. Masaru Emoto and Professor Luc Montagnier, to name a few, have conducted tests on water and how this memory can be stored in it. They observed under the microscope the shape water molecules take after being subjected to different types of outside stimuli, such as someone expressing love, hate, and gratitude to water over a certain time. They studied the impacts of stimuli on atomic and molecular levels of water and the shape each stimulus took when water was frozen suddenly. Only if we think of the fact that our bodies are made of 70% water should let us wonder about our exact nature. This experiment shows how we can communicate even with water or any element through memory particle exchange.

This memory storage ability applies to every existing thing in our Universe on the atomic level to variant degrees. As discussed earlier, any two elements can exchange memory information between them through magnetism, electricity, vibrations, and frequencies. The information, when stored, remains as-is for life unless re-imprinted on top with new memory. Other elements do not have enough electricity to imprint as we do. Therefore, they cannot store a lot of sensory memory or can store minimal sensory memory for a very short span. But whatever sensory memory ability they can store, genetic memory, and running memory are always imprinted in these elements at all levels.

What is around us gets imprinted in many ways, but all by the exchange of information stored in the memory particles. Heat, which is generated by the higher vibration of atoms, imprints whatever it surrounds. It does so by exchanging the memory with the atoms around it, like water, air, or others. The vibrations of the heat are higher, so it has a stronger effect on what surrounds it and imprints it. However, if you increase the vibration around this heat to a level higher than the heat vibrations, the heat itself will get imprinted by the memory around it. Therefore, imprinting happens through gaining higher or lower vibrations on all other memory levels.

To put it simply, if we keep filling the mind and body with negativity, it will soon imprint the whole body, erasing every ounce of positivity. Increasing the vibrations of negativity leads to information exchange between memory particles, which leads to multiplied negativity across our bodies. Therefore, we must ensure on conscious levels the type of memory we store throughout our life. Be mindful that our body is not a brain-controlled single entity, rather a collection of 60 trillion cells with defined atoms and memory entities. On a smaller level, each cell in our body is made of around 100 trillion atoms, with each atom having its memory. And to complicate a bit of the matter to have an idea of what you are dealing with on these particles level, one atom contains around 150 trillion of a trillion of pure memory particles. The number of stars in the Milky Way, for instance, is around 300 billion, so the number of stars in the Milky Way, which is our entire galaxy and seems unlimited to us, is a tiny dot number-wise given the number of cells in a single human body. Thus, we are internally bigger and more complex inside on our cellular level than our Universe or what has been discovered so far out of it.

Having as many memory particles multiplied by the total number of atoms and cells can give you an idea of how much memory capacity we contain therein and wonder on the real capabilities we can acquire and compare it to what we are putting at work and for what purpose. Moreover, one can imagine how little we still have imprinted ourselves, and how much more we can. Trying to imagine this would surely leave anyone trying to imagine it blank, and speechless for hours in front of such a creation. This is only one of us, if you take it to the human level, this would be infinity, and if you imagine the memory particles floating in the air, our environment, the atmosphere, and what mistakenly believe as emptiness, you could realize the complexity and immensity of this unlimited memory particles world, and how memory spreads across everything all the time.

What makes us more distinct from other creatures is that while most of them can store memory and emit it up to a certain level, we can store and emit back an unlimited amount of this memory to any element we choose. In return, we get memory from any other element in our environment and ultimately "The source," which is the main memory we should focus on, as it is the purest. Our complicated electrical system mechanism makes it all possible, which is beyond any creature's or element. Electricity in our cells, our organs, heart, etc., is carried out by the brain, which is the ultimate organizer and reader of all information of all our memories. It is also responsible for carrying, transporting, reading, and imprinting memory particles. The unlimited ability we have is because we can vibrate on any level of energy we choose to, and the electricity conducts have been more effective due to higher frequencies arising out of these vibrations. Thus, our more complex reader and transmitter of this memory, the brain, and its constituents as well as all other organs and even our atoms are more evolved and developed than in any other living being, which allows much higher levels of imprinting, reading, and storage.

One can imagine at this very tiny level yet unlimited in volume how much energy a single thought, word, or action can generate in our Universe, just looking at the number of particles that are contained in one single thought or action and what we are putting at work.

The same memory particles can take many forms depending on their imprinting and number when gathering together, and their unity and imprinting determine the type of atom they model and form. How these atoms are connected and gathered determines the nature and purpose of any element or creature. Our atoms are by default imprinted with Divine, Running, Genetic, and Still memories.

The closest we get to "The Source," the strongest and more effective this memory becomes as it is accessed at a purer level with less sensory imprinting. Sensory imprinting is the key to allow us to experience this memory. The less imprinting of sensory memory, the more the chances of reaching higher memories and thus the source. However, it is effective in directing us towards the social and natural environment. Setting a direct channel for a determined purpose towards a higher source is vital in any endeavor, as this channel allows its materialization. But this memory obtained from higher levels should be received and shaped properly to become sensory memory with correct imprinting with positive energy and pureness for it to prosper and be productive.

Once sensory memory is added to the variety of basic purer memories in the atom, cell, or organ, it will directly start to exchange the information contained in it with the other particles through electric signals similar as in a reverse diffusion. It should be added in conformity with the nature of pure memory, and this is why one must free his thoughts of all pollutants before leading this new experience as we can imagine the effects and results of just storing anything that comes our way in a random, unfiltered manner.

Filtering, hence, is an essential principle of the imprinting process. It helps us figure out only the creative and prolific ideas, images, and experiences while multiplying and flourishing them. It is similar to going to the grocery store where you do not just buy the whole store; you buy what you need based on what you have set to do already in your mind.

Positivity and happiness, when gathered,

require nourishment and maintenance through acquiring it daily. We need to filter the unaligned ideas, thoughts, experiences, and actions through conscious rationalization or avoidance. One should always look for what any involvement can and would add to his life and whether it goes with his broader vision or not before experiencing it.

With adequate time, the filtering mechanism becomes innate. It lets the individual deal with any situation that arises immediately, as to whether he should be involved in it or make it part of his experience or not. If one is, however, looking on the contrary for misery, he could reverse the process to accumulate anything that comes his way. Therefore, setting a general direction in the beginning for where you intend to be, is imprinting at the highest level and is a must.

I suggest that one starts by writing down on a piece of paper his current life direction as well as whatever happens each day.

On another piece of paper, write down how you want your life to be and whatever needs to be done to achieve it, and now start writing down all that happens or think of in the corresponding paper. Does this belong to the life I want or the life I have? Some might fall under both papers, but the segregation will show you that you are mostly not applying what you look for in your daily actions. If the details on each paper are different, that means you are leading a life that you do not want or do not deserve.

This process will allow one to have a conscious objective view of where he is heading. Therefore, the process will allow you to choose between the two willfully. We cannot have the life we want unless we leave behind broken things in the current life we lead or work on fixing them. It allows for rational and detailed scrutiny, which improves your perspectives and enables the implementation of the vision. Bear in mind, whatever goes on within, get an amplified projection to the outside. No matter what we do, we will keep attracting more of it. Therefore, if we are unhappy at one stage with our lives or find ourselves defective in our relationships, it is directly due to what we have been working unconsciously on imprinting ourselves with at an earlier stage, whatever it is whether due to actions, accidents, or traumas.

Furthermore, setting-up visions such as becoming successful and better off and applying this vision in a Machiavellian way might lead to our vision being achieved in a way with negative actions. But the ways contradict the end goal, and thus the means would have been so cruelly unethical, and negative to the extent that will never let you enjoy later the fruits of your success which will always be subject to collapse as whatever you have put into your efforts, is so destructive.

What you put in the equation of existence gets back to you, multiplied. It is not an equation or philosophy to be learned by heart, rather the absolute of our existence, which demands respect. All get registered on the memory level even when no one is watching. Thinking otherwise would be the result of a defective blind mind that must revisit itself.

We should never plant an apple seed and expect to get a fully-grown orange tree out of it. It is not also a who is a smarter game to play with this memory and try to trick it and believe no one is watching because this memory is us and we are it and is also all that is around us, and this is not a game. What happens in us happens in all memory around us and is accessible maybe not by some around us at the spot, but things will always get visible at a certain point because of this registry.

Trying to fool people around us to get our vision accomplished is like building our significant monument that we want it to last for ages with paper. It might look good from the outside for a short period once accomplished but is surely doomed to collapse very shortly. This wrong imprinting through wrong actions is useless and would only consume our time and energy for nothing, so it is better to do nothing than apply such planning into our lives. Moreover, if accomplishing your vision requires contributions from others, ensure the grounds of values are shared among the group, including ethics, morals, and beliefs. Otherwise, the vision is doomed to fail as the combined memory recorded is negative, although ours is pure and clear. This is because negativity has more impact on memory; thus, negative imprinting is stronger due to higher vibrations, even if it is for shorter spans. This fact does not only apply to visions, rather to everything we are looking to live or build, be it a career, relation or marriage. Many people fail in realizing their visions, not because of their actions and devotion, but because they involved the wrong people in them. Therefore, imprinting is done at the individual level and at the group level irrespective of our consideration of this vision.

Therefore, when setting goals or implementing the vision, make sure to do your part with due diligence. Check all the variables related to the work and add them up to find the possibility of achieving goals. Rely on goals in line with the Universe's laws, study the natural process, and leverage the sensory memory to understand nature in its simplest form. One should do that as many times as possible to remove all uncertainties. All visions, being major imprinting, require you to have certain qualities to be fulfilled. I learned a lot from trees, as they stand tall, robust, and firm irrespective of what happens around them. They have in place a big root system, which anchors them to the ground and allows them to gather nutrients in silence. A tree at a seed level did not spend its time stressing on how to become a tree, how to look like on the outside but rather facilitated the process of it growing naturally the way it should and our life should be simplified to this level to be productive and give more fruits.

These qualities are what is available in the pure memory of the source, allowing the proper flourishing of genetic memory. The process should be carefully understood before adding up our sensory memories, general knowledge, and actions to the recipe.

Thus, returning to the simplicity like in pure memory is a must and should be everyone's goal. It enhances the quality of life and allows us to experience the real joy in it whilst letting in only external stimuli in line with his well-being.

As the pure source memory filters out everything, filling your life with prosperity, the right track for a fulfilling life will be set. One can sense its impact both inside and outside himself, as it changes the attitudes and actions towards things. By that, he will spare himself a lot of arguments, avoid unnecessary problems, focus on things that need his attention, and differentiate between what is productive and what is not. The value of his living would increase. Once this state of mind is reached, the sky becomes the limit. The human body and brain will gain unlimited potentials to do even miracles when adjusting to this new reality.

Aligning all different memories in our body in one direction is essential as, without this alignment, it becomes a real inconvenience to achieve any action, even the smallest. When memories are not in line, one can feel a certain unease in doing anything even if he believes they are the right things to do and would prefer to adjourn rather than act. Procrastination is just one form of the excuses used when these memories are not aligned; this is because memories do not feel at ease in the body when someone forces them to clash due to opposite imprinting. Thus, they give you the feeling of doing nothing rather than putting them in an unpleasant confrontational scenario. So, taming the genetic memory and the fight and flight responses generated from it and leaving more space for the pure memory and the right sensory memory that we filtered will help us in that lining-up process. Taming your genetic memory is done by imprinting it with conscious behavior and letting all that's aware that we are in control of our survival mode, thus setting new rules and laws within.

After doing that, one realizes how organized internally he becomes in the sense that nothing is left to dictate by itself, which gets imprinted in the genetic memory. Attending to our genetic memory is a delicate task. Where we need to for survival, it is also necessary to have control over it in case genetic memory is the only source of reliance. They would compare to a wild lion getting unleashed inside, without even having the slightest control over him.

Pure memory exists in us, as well as obtained constantly from the source directly or through elements. Eating, breathing, experiencing, socializing, thinking, and to a larger extent, acting, in general, are all ways to receive pure memory, with different levels of imprinting. The majority of sensory memory, when received fades, genetic memory and the pure memory particles, remain and become an addition to us where they get imprinted by us. However, direct memory obtained from the source when joining in they do the imprinting on us. The way that works is rather than an electric circuit conducts the particles through us, vibrations and frequencies do this job along with electricity. Thus, the imprinting is more strong. So unlike particles emanating from our five senses and our thinking process, these particles reach the mind directly and get diffused in the body. Unlike having an accident or getting injured, or eating food, pure memory is from the source. It is the only memory that exerts direct imprinting in our thinking process: the brain and all nerves connected to it. So, the source's energy can be imprinted in any element at specific frequencies and vibrations without being subject to filtering. All memory can be partially or deleted depending on the external stimuli' power except pure memory as it constitutes everything. Thus, it affects all and never gets affected by anything because anything is it. A nuclear bomb can delete all memory within a specific circumference and turn it into pure memory dispersed by the explosion's frequency and vibration.

However, on the particle level, nothing is lost. What is lost is only the associations of what was there before the explosion. The shift in memory from frequency to vibration to electricity can be observed in some elements, like the change of state of water. When water turns to gas or turns to solid depending on the frequency and vibration, we subject it to, at that instance, heat breaks memory associations into smaller units or let them accumulate more memory depending on the scenario.

Association and dissociation of memory happen daily in our lives, without us even noticing it. Even on the mental level, that includes thoughts, and this is mainly due to imprinting and the forces in the pure memory particles that make this imprinting possible. However, the imprinting we consciously carry out is imprinting on previous information. Such information is unfiltered and received chaotically, making it indirect partial imprinting through fragmented information. These fragments of information are gathered from news, social media, and films, along with the food we consume. Every day we are served with junk memory in breakfast, lunch, and dinner while imprinting our unconscious memory. Experiences such as love, kindness, and good deeds should be the ones getting imprinted. We carry out these actions in our memory. Although we have not experienced them and this is the reason behind detoxification of the mind from any prior knowledge.

Some of us watch a movie about a person who is so kind to others and helps people out. We usually associate it to actions we might do, and at the end of the film, we would have a good feeling. It develops feelings about how kind we are and what good we are doing. We start believing we are good people, whilst we did nothing, neither good nor bad.

Because of this partial imprinting mechanism that we introduced in our lives and which we are subjected to every day, we believe that we are the best in whatever we do. We are the nicest, kindest, rightest, most fair people as a result of such imprinting. We can just objectively on a certain day wonder about any good action we have done for this day or during the last couple of days, even weeks or months, and the answer could shock us. It might be nothing or too little at a time when we feel we are the kindest and most caring people ever.

Another danger of applying our partial passive imprinting into our lives is its inaccuracy. For example, we walked down the street and heard a certain person shouting like crazy at another one, so we continued our walk thinking what a mad person we just saw; this man must surely be irrational. We now have imprinted our memory with the scene and the idea that we have seen a crazy man going nuts. What if later we the truth about the person dawn on us? What if he was a well-respected person of the neighborhood shouting at a mentally unstable man for torturing his cat, harassing his daughter, and attempting robbery? On discovering that your perception would not remain the same until you know the full story.

On a marginal note, like we said before and would like to stress more on it, all psychological problems are linked to our lives' scenarios and how we perceive the reality of those occurrences. Essentially, it depends on how our brain reads these experiences and creates the belief that only these are true; it could be unorganized and chaotic. When we keep subjecting our minds to these partial realities and consider them as facts, for long periods, the process turns into thinking habits and later prejudgments to become our character which will determine our actions and will define our individual life and where it heads.

Another issue that we can face while gathering information is subjectivity and prior conditioning. It could be direct, derived from stored data on a sensory and genetic level, or indirect, extracted from life experiences. It all depends on the relevance of the situation.

For example, we have four creatures, an elephant, a lion, and an ant, and a human on the same field. For the elephant, his main concern is either the lion he is watching closely as the lion sees him as lunch or the human because, at one point, a human might have tried to harm him, and he kept a bad memory of that incident. The human could, from his perspective, fear the lion's presence as he has memories, both on the genetic level or sensory levels (like watching a movie or documentary) or through direct experience, that lions attack humans. The lion could look at all with a look that no one is safe here. The ant might care less about all others as it is unnoticed by everyone around. Memory at this stage makes everyone secrete different hormones in their respective bodies. The human can flee, the lion can attack the elephant if he chooses to, and the ant can be careless of what happens.

This is imprinting put into action and relies solely on the way our memory was conditioned. What happened in that scenario is that at this exact moment where all four men on the same site, the lion had just eaten, so he has no interest whatsoever in attacking anything. He just needs to rest. The human had encountered a lion before and dared to fight the lion and not flee.

On the other hand, the elephant leaves the site, and while proceeding with his way, steps unintentionally on the ant and smashes it. This shows that imprinting is a constant accumulation of information on all levels, not to be done for a short time. Being satisfied with knowing one thing without updating our knowledge would render it useless, which is why we should look to understand the whole picture.

Moreover, what one can realize on the memories' web level, is the powers all memories try to exert on each other outside this still memory realm and at the still memory level at a lesser extent and in us the least. The stronger the memory is, the more effective it will be on this web. Genetic memory relies mainly on the survival of the fittest. It can exert a lot of control when combined with different memories in humans, animals, viruses, bacteria, or any living organism. A bacterium can take over the body and kill it by duplicating and transiting its memory between each other, duping the host's defense mechanism and weakening to achieve the purpose. For us, this could be a disaster and would, for sure, surely cause this bacterium as harmful, but for the bacteria, it is a must to survive and ensure its existence. This show of will powers between memories is not subject to right or wrong. It is subject to a very clear and simple equation, which is killed or be killed, and this would subject the memory relying on genetic conditioning alone. Beings or organisms relying on genetic memory have very short life cycles.

The survival mechanism is not a reliable survival instrument by itself in this context as it shortly will lead to one's demise and dissociation of memory. Therefore, with pure and a lot of correct sensory memory learned from experiences and creating proper survival tools, imprinting genetic memory is a must. Even the fiercest lion's genetic memory is constantly being imprinted by sensory memory through experiences and thoughts to a certain level, although to a lesser extent than in humans.

Therefore, transcending in this imprinting is crucial to be able to distort this memory web around us and shape it in our favor for us to have long-term fruitful objectives.

The deeper the transcendence in high-level memory imprinting, the more conscious he will become of good and bad concepts. The actions would be less dependent on the genetic memory, drawing him closer to Divine memory. One will lose some addictions, some phobias, and a lot of fear and hesitation he had in his life during this process. Even his character and actions will change for the better.

The proper way to imprint our pure memory is by applying objectivity in the process. Doing so requires an understanding that any scenario can be possible since all that we know could be partial if it were not rightly implemented at first.

Objectivity, while imprinting our unconscious with pure memory or adding on our cells' memory, is understanding that the experience you have been subjected to is not the only possibility in life; rather, it is one in an unlimited number of possibilities. That is why relying only on branded memory is dangerous. We should rely on some other memories; whose existence is not in our knowledge. Such a memory is always in contact with us through various channels, but we humans are usually bad listeners. Listening to your hunch and heart and gut feelings in dealing with anything plays a significant role in life. It emanates directly from the pure memory, which is either stored in what surrounds us or in us and can be accessed consciously on the spot in every situation if you choose to do so.

Try clearing your mind when encountering a problem, have a moment of silence, and listen to the answer in your heart. It would most of the time flash in your heart. Write it down and revisit it later, and you would see most of what you wrote was correct.

That is when knowledge and comprehensibility of the idea become crucial in the imprinting process. You should be objective and open to different possibilities, relying on the freshly received information and not the stored one. It could be so that the stored information might have been remodeled multiple times into different scenarios.

The correct way to do it is through gathering the pieces of memory from the correct and direct sources. Putting together and organizing all these pieces together to form the correct memory with which you should imprint your unconscious memory with a big concentration on unconscious flashes. It is what I believe is more conscious than what we usually refer to consciousness. The unconscious is more conscious than our consciousness, but we do not train ourselves to read, nor can we read because it is a part of higher memory.

Relying on hunches can be a good door to open the first door in reading it.

So, the shift occurs inside of you before happening on the outside. The shift in dealing with internal storage, organizing it, and removing all polluted or partial memory that negatively affects us, enables us to become a magnet to attract anything positive we seek in our life. It tells us a lot about the Universe's laws, laws of actions, reaping and sowing laws, and laws of attraction. It serves as the cornerstone in building what we desire, attracting it through reverse imprinting.

Once we get the idea that everything we thought of as being true in our life could be not true and could be a partial and just a small detail in a bigger picture is when proper imprinting and reverse imprinting occur.

At this stage, all memory should be revisited by our thoughts to become for some organization. Little by little, a bigger, more meaningful understanding of the reality of things would begin to form once memory gets a bit more organized and not left at its chaotic state. We mostly have used our thoughts to build walls and not bridges.

Therefore, we must use the memory to build connections by keeping the flow of memory within us similar to the water flow, ready to take the shape of the river or any other form. We should never deal with this memory we are building as rigid conceptual facts, as it is not so in essence.

If we do, this would have a big backfiring effect on us, collapse everything we have built, and make us prisoners sentenced to death by our thoughts. The imprinting stage should occur as it happens in a child, i.e., without too much effort and as it was something new, keeping in mind always the filtering process. For sure, we will have to filter it more lately, but the attitude should always be imprinted now and erase whatever is always not needed later whilst keeping the main filter present.

Therefore, after waking up and showing gratitude that we are still alive, we should start focusing on the idea of how much we can do today to positively add up to our memory and self. When taking that stance, we would shortly discover that we can focus more on things, listen better to people and judge less.

I always try to portray myself as a big sponge, ready to slurp all water in. Where it helps you acquire control over thoughts and feelings, it also enables you to master control over it.

Soon, you will realize that what surrounds you can be controlled in a certain way. In return, it helps in reducing the external impacts of experiences, people, and reflection of their memory onto us.

A good listener is a good judge of figuring out from where people come. The consciousness of it allows us to get rid of most of our ego's bad parts, building a new and more objective individual. Such an individual is aware that people's opinions or judgments are never related to you but are a reflection of who they are. Starting to imprint our pure memory with this logic and with this new way of looking at things will take our human unconscious behavior and thoughts to a new, more conscious pleasant level.

I believe that it is because this reduces the stress hormones in our bodies and that in return plays a significant role in feeling better and more relaxed.

Understanding the motives behind anyone's negative attitude towards us allows us to distance ourselves from being said or expressed. At this stage, we become more conscious of others' motives and how things work within us. Therefore, when you properly imprint and organize memory, life will be so much different in time, our character will be different, our relations will be different, our logic, our judgment, our thoughts, our EGO all will be better versions of what they are.

This imprinting in us will be so strong, to the point that our reality will change, and so will be our priorities which will be more targeted and specific with more torque to it. This is Karma in its ultimate manifestation. We become true magnets through what we have implemented and will attract people, events in our life that are similar in nature.

When imprinted directly from the source, the pure memory has the source intelligence and data, which is beyond our comprehension. The information is not contaminated with genetic data, like the memory in our bodies. So, when receiving it, at times, the brain manages to read some of this information, the reason we experience hunches, gut feeling, and the sixth sense capabilities some people have. These states of mind and abilities are usually us reading this real data unknowingly. Focusing on these occurrences when it happens can teach us to properly read these signals and be able to decipher the fading memory they contain. These happenings contain the key and directions to materialize things and get more aware of the reality of things as usually they contain the truth with no veils. When you see the tip of the iceberg in this and start to dig further into it, is when the laws of attraction will start to get revealed. Therefore, attracting this memory and imprinting it in us will erase contaminated memory and help us gain new powers that are beyond us and the ability to generate through our actions and thoughts things that were impossible before and generate ideas we never thought exist.

The imprinting phase should always be followed by a still phase for all laws to work; we cannot keep the process going on all the time. We are applying this so we can properly use it in our favor. After storing adequate amounts of pure memory or imprinting old memory, phases of stillness and contemplation on whatever we gathered should follow. We are bound at this stage to consider life's complex simplicity. Focusing on breathing and trying to make it as conscious as possible while feeling it relax is necessary to let all the memory settle in. The process of breathing in a still state allows the memory to get organized. The organized memory is then spread by electricity in our bodies and emitted out as frequencies, vibrations, and magnetic sharing of charges.

The pure memory subjects our atoms to new laws and information it contains by adding higher vibrations. Thus, reflecting on this accumulation as a daily routine will elevate us to more advanced existentialist heights while allowing necessary changes to occur for our further and broader development. Although on the genetic level, this happens automatically and can be noticed by looking at our 10-year-old picture and recognizing ourselves in it. The body altogether and all its cells have been renewed, and not even one cell of what we see in the old picture still exists on the sensory level. However, it needs full devotion and awareness, and practice to reflect full edge buildup. A deep reflection on this imprinting, memory exchange, and stockpiling would introduce us to a new concept of time. It enables us to note that time as we know it does not actually exist but is rather the direct result of memory accumulation in an organized manner. It triggers a feeling of change, giving us an explanation of how things are different from before.

What we invented as time is an attempt to frame memory and try to show in a particular manner this memory accumulation, evolution, and accuracy. Although a day on earth is made of 24 hours, a day on other planets like Venus is around 6,000 hours and would be much less elsewhere, and our lifespan could be just a few days there, but this does not mean we live shorter on Venus or elsewhere as the accumulation everywhere is the same. It is like being dead at birth elsewhere for a fly that lives 40 days by our set time. Time is, in fact, the accumulation of memory needed for any element to achieve what it was designed for and thus determines its lifespan.

Accumulation is a long process as it is done systematically with certain limitations and is, in fact, a never-ending process. At a certain time in life, I used to believe that to have a positive change in life through knowledge, and one should be familiar with universal laws. I thought that one should wake up, show gratitude, ask for change, and the next day it will be presented to us. The fact is unless you are the luckiest person in the Universe, this will never happen this way. Certainly, this is one very minimal side in these laws, but it is so minimal that it hardly affects us or the laws, so how can it affect the Universe around us. Only memory accumulation and binding them in your favor could initiate change. Gratitude to an extent and the desire to another extent are a beginning but they are not the way used alone, as more stamina is needed for the shift to occur. However, their presence in the process is crucial.

Before, one should fix the machine inside and make it work to enable it to accomplish tasks for him. Here comes the necessity of starting to incorporate all this already explained behavior and mechanism to regulate the machine. For this purpose, we should rely on several tools to make things happen, mainly repetition. There is a lot of imprinting power in repetition, failing, and trying again, as when we write on our memory, delete it, write again, delete some…, we become our life editors.

Sometimes you will have to repeat some ideas or some actions thousands of times before seeing any result. The other tool which will empower us is writing things down somewhere, ideas, wishes, dreams, experiences, whatever comes to our mind. Sometimes, the greatest idea and most valuable information reach our brains and leave before capturing it because of daily life activities and distractions, as noted earlier.

I suggest keeping a particular book note at reach for this purpose. Reading what we have written, from time to time, can reveal a lot to dig in right there later.

The other benefit of this is that it allows you to imprint your memory at other places, so now you also have the same idea in you in the world.

First, this confirms to the world that this idea is worth looking at as it exists imprinted at many places and increases its magnetism. Second, this allows us to distance ourselves from our thoughts or ideas and look at them more objectively.

The imprinting mechanism is in this way like planting all around us and within us receptors and emitters at certain frequencies to send or capture the memory. The more we succeed in obtaining the right frequencies, the stronger the signal emitted or received is. It is the most important aspect you can choose what to send, where to send, and what to receive, and from where to receive in a very clear coding. This is the main process to recreate whatever you choose to. Eliminating all the bad frequencies that are of no good to us, we can remodel ourselves, assembling all the good frequencies to reach higher objectives.

The two types of imprinting that happen in our body, both writing on existing memory and replacing parts of memory particles in our atoms, are crucial for implementing a successful life. The procedure is not a day's practice rather a way of living that reflects on our external factors. One of the greatest impacts on genetic levels is a healthier and less stressed life. It has nothing to do with becoming a mystic or a person always isolating himself. One can continue to live his life as is but have superior actions and considerations that will reflect his choices, beliefs, ethics, actions, and all that come with it and change him for the best. The process takes a while because of the extensive need for accumulation for change to occur. As we comprise some sixty billion camps (cells), with few trillions of soldiers (memory particles) in each, to feed, train and ensure they follow the direction we set requires huge efforts. The good part of it is that a lot of these soldiers are self-disciplined and know precisely what to do by already being imprinted with genetic memory with all traces of higher memories and run by our unconscious.

After any imprinting, maintenance work at all-time should be carried out to keep the imprinting. The memory stays as is if not subjected to different memories, but our existence is subject to continuous association and dissociation of all kinds of memories. One should become aware of ways to protect this stamping and not only through filtering as filtering allows the right memory to get in but once in a big conservation job is to be done.

Take addiction; for instance, it would reverse the imprinting we have done so far with a multitude of memories.

Once the substance becomes a part of genetic memory and cell, it programs it and starts working parallel to it. Therefore, addictions play a major role in making a big part of our inside soldiers defect, and join the substance memory. Addictions are the most difficult memories to overcome because the information in the memory they hold is condensed. Therefore, they are so hard to overcome unless one finds a stronger memory to fight them. Sports can help, the psychological treatment also can, but not to introduce them to our bodies in the first place is the best way as they could affect to a big extent our main imprinting strategy and take it from organized and conscious to a chaotic unconscious path.

The proper imprinting for food and any substance which gets in your body should be drawn from nature as available there without alteration as it is one of the purest forms of memory available.

Thus, one might notice that he is not really what he ought to think he is, but rather what is stored in a memory, whether being from the environment or other memory sources, as without memory, we and our environment would not exist.

To elaborate a bit on that, one can imagine a car crash, where we and the car are left with bad memories. The car will be permanently damaged, keeping the shape of the strong vibrations it got subjected to. These vibrations resulting from the frequency at which the car was moving when hitting another frequency, which can be a wall in that instance, will change the wall and the car's memory.

After this shift in frequency and vibrations, elements try to return to the closest of their prior vibration level. The vibration subsides but registers the corresponding memory everywhere it was present. New memory has been stored in the wall, and the car after the vibrations subsided and the new imprinting will remain in this state until subjected to new frequencies that alter their memory again.

This is imprinting in its most concrete form. So, unless we take the car to the garage to get it fixed by applying the required vibrations on the damaged area, the vehicle would stay in its new state of last recorded memory. The car's memory cannot be altered by itself, but for us processing the accident in our brain and body can result in imprinting the memory of the accident as we desire by applying all kinds of frequencies and vibrations through the electric power in our body. We can even choose to work completely on deleting the experience altogether, and this is how powerful is our imprinting mechanism.

Our ability to model our general memory and reality into whatever nature we choose is an edge we have on all creatures and elements around us. We can imprint and re-imprint our pure memory with so many experiences and thoughts and keep these memories as such for a lifetime.

We can delete memory through the consciousness, and we can write memory through it, and one way to do it is by thinking more deeply more often of what we are experiencing. However, although unlimited, thinking as a process should work along with our senses and our unconscious memory to be effective. This unconscious memory, which some people describe as a subconscious mind, although I don't agree with the terminology as it is not limited to our minds only, rather it is related to all atoms in our body, which are and are processed by the mind. It is critical to our thinking process, even though most see it as a danger and risk. It is responsible for the flow of electricity in the synopsis from all parts to the brain and vice versa and for keeping the thinking process running when we are not using our consciousness. It is based on what we are, but we cannot operate even on the basic level without it.

The above being said, our success in life, our advancement, reaching our goals relies on how we build this memory, organize it, group it on all levels, and communicate it to our environment and the Universe. If we think about this a bit, we would realize that it is like a puzzle game, where every piece matters. It should be put together in an organized manner to get the full picture, but it is difficult to perceive the picture we are trying to complete when scattered. Adding knowledge bit by bit and piece by piece will soon reveal the whole picture to anyone.

Memory at the source cannot be used as-is on a conscious level, as it is still pure and lower in frequency and vibrations. It needs to be subjected to higher frequencies and vibration to work, so imprinting is crucial. The memory is used on the biological level as genetic memory.

After that, it is regarded as sensory memory where its vibrations are elevated to readable and operational levels. It is triggered by the source frequency and is imprinted with a specific vibration level to have it activated on the cosmos level. It is mainly imprinted at the source by Divine memory.

The primary type a human can experience in an obvious manner is the genetic memory responsible for developing the fetus and establishing our unconscious memory so we can be formed. Electricity, which is a form of vibration, is crucial at this stage, as if the ovule is charged positively, it will attract the sperms charged negatively, so the half imprinting of each will unite and form the first cell that has the first type of memory we experience. This genetic memory is turned whilst the fetus is being formed into unconscious memory to form the cells by division and later the organs until the full unconscious memory reveals in a human who has in him the memory necessary for future breeding.

So electricity is crucial in the memory imprinting process, and this is why our 50 trillion cells, charged with around 0.7 to 2 volts each matter, as this combined is crucial to extract a memory from the source and plays the major role in the imprinting of memory with information to turn it to other types of memory. Not all can be imprinted to any kind of our chosen memory.

The type of memory to be imprinted differs from cell to cell; however, all can be imprinted with genetic memory. The above being said, we need to understand how important the sensory memory imprinting on the pure memory to our lives is because this is what determines the quality and nature of our human experience and connection with the outside.

We should always control our breathing and make it conscious of being able to have this process running smoothly inside of us. This will allow whatever stored conscious memory to run through us and build the proper connections throughout your system and regulate your body, to be aligned with all energies available by all memories around us. Stillness is a key in letting this memory set in us, releasing its true effectiveness. As memory tends to fade and get imprinted by the unconscious with our survival memory information, we let it go this way. The most conscious state of mind we can reach is when we allow these times of meditation-like moments where we reflect on our surroundings and let it reflect on us, cutting off all external stimuli with very high vibrations and just focusing on what gets from our insides out.

We should also realize the memory we imprinted our bodies with, up to this point, is a product of limited senses. Therefore, this memory is a small part of what is available to access, and there is more to it than what we believe, think, and reach. It requires conviction within us that all we know in our life is little as knowledge out there is unlimited. Unless we get convinced of that, we are using it to build a wall around us that keeps us away from reality.

Problems will still be present at all levels in our life, but we will gain the ability to know how to deal with them and know that anything can be resolved when we choose to do so. This reality will give anyone more power and a feeling of being protected by the whole system in place. When we start living in a world where we feel like wearing a shield arising of this power which gets built little by knowing we are directly connected to a higher authority and that nothing is lost rather reshaped.

We should always seek this source and contemplate its entireness and unlimited powers, being stronger than whatever is out there.

Whatever is out there, has a fraction of it, which will give you the recognition that a will can within this existence defeat anything when it decides to do so as the external imprinting will be stronger than anything at this level.

Another thing is that fears, phobias, negativity in our life are all imaginary and by giving way to this new dimension we never dreamed exists, a feeling of prosperity and gratitude like no other would always follow.

If maintained properly by feeding it up with the right ingredients, the new memory will remove all burdens from our life and bring good to it irrespective of any situation, whether good or bad. Even if the situation is so bad, impacting it by your positively charged memory will alter the memory of the situation and the people who are creating it.

However, in some situations depending on the nature of impacted negative memory, the proper imprinting will have minimal effects if not carried out properly long enough. That's when our hunch will tell us what to do until adequate imprinting is completed since strong imprinting requires a lot of energy to alter. Sometimes, we need to remove a lot of people from our lives and create a new environment for ourselves to succeed. Another form of bad imprinting is a disease, as it creates an imbalance in the body's memory. Our body doesn't know how to fight the invaders since these intelligent invaders shift tactics to win over the body's defense mechanism. We might not have the proper knowledge or will to fight them. Thus, other memories of the intruding agents prevail.

Once we know what is causing the imbalance and once one gets the conscious memory of what that imbalance is and how it occurs, beating it is inevitable no matter what the illness is, just by directing our energy towards it and making our memory conquer. Most diseases have parasites as root causes and have a big role in letting viruses and bacteria proliferate. The lack of imprinting of what the disease is in our immune system due to the lack of genetic memory of what the disease is and the help we offer to these intruders arising from our lack of knowledge and surrender allows it to thrive.

The most lethal scenario is when parasites become systemic and suck the nutrients needed by our memory to work properly. It drains the immune system and subjects our body to the authority and will of the invading disease while our body surrenders to the will of the imprinting of the disease. Our body starts providing it with what it feeds on, like sugar, negativity, fear, weakness, etc. So, we become like a car running on the wrong fuel, ineffective and dying off, and this is the major cause that leads to severe conditions like cancer and so many other critical illnesses.

We generally tend to describe any illness or unease in the body as disease, but most diseases do not kill us but rather are beneficial to our survival from an immune point of view. The diseases that kill are the diseases one allows to build up over a long period by unconsciously helping the disease ourselves without marking it to get rid of it.

Thus, we render the disease stronger than our cells. Having adequate information on the disease and its nature allows the body to acquire enough energy to fight it. The energy permeates the cell level, giving control to the immune system and cutting off the necessities of disease. As soon as the imprinting process starts to be implemented correctly at all body levels, one could realize that his nature and his dealing with the outside is changing, and the power behind life motor starts to reveal itself more and more.

At this stage, one could get a real sense that it is possible to access and read memory stored in others, understand their feelings, and experience events that are going to happen. All these are memories stored around us in the environment and Universe in different imprinting at different levels. One's life could turn into a real manifestation of human power and sixth sense, and other abilities would be more developed.

Wondering about this power that rules and models all these particles and the energies behind them become an unavoidable result.

FIVE

THE SOURCE AND HOW TO ACCESS IT

REACHING OUT FOR "The Source" is not attaining a definite place far away in the Universe, but rather acquiring a new ability to read and communicate in silence with the existence as a whole, through "pure memory" inside us. Pure memory particles are the closest someone will ever be able to get to creation as all that's behind it is unattainable by what's physical. "The Source," where anything physical is born, is a vast power that generates life and all its components. You should be ready to start receiving the source energy from all that surrounds you at different levels from everything. This ability is the key to unlocking one's life in all its meanings. All that constitutes us and surrounds us is made from the accumulation

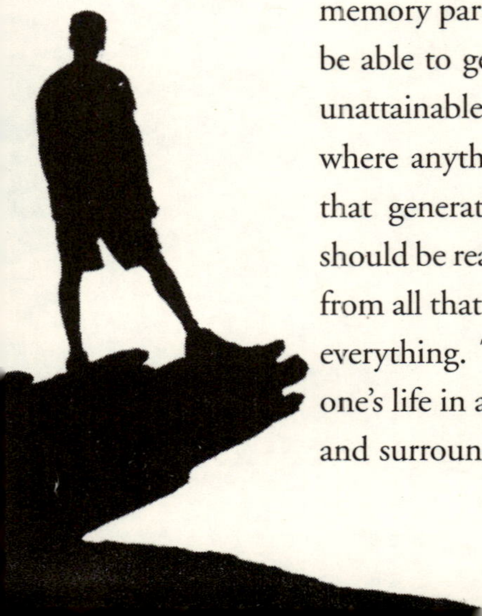

of different memory forms, made of pure memory particles. These memory particles are constituents of all that you can see or cannot see. Before being imprinted with any type of information, they are in the primary purest form.

All elements in the Universe and all life forms are formed by different associations and formations of memory particles imprinted with unlimited numbers of information, through information exchange between each particle of the formation and the whole (other particles and the environment) and all generated from pure memory.

After getting imprinted with new data by other particles, the particle gains new imprinting, and it stays so until another stronger memory imprints something additional on top of its data. Air molecules around us, which is a certain type of association of this memory imprinted to become oxygen, nitrogen, etc., all float in a sea of unseen free particle worlds of this pure memory. This pure memory occupies 100% of the space, being the constituent of both the air molecules in essence and all the particles where the atoms float, which we mistakenly believe is empty around them, go unseen and unfelt as they sit weightlessly and have extremely minute sizes beyond imagination.

Research has reached so far, the "Planck" level (named after Physicist Max Planck). Plancks are subatomic particles 7 levels below our known atomic level. These pure memory particles which are the primary base of life gather in billions to form even one Planck.

It is very hard at our existence level to even realize they even exist, but the reality is that nothing around us is void or empty. Everything in us and around us is filled and formed by an indefinite number of "pure memory" particles to the extent that the whole Universe, what we see of it or cannot see, is floating in this matter to form an endless tissue that occupies the whole Universe in all directions.

The best way to realize their existence in their original form is by checking the areas in the Universe where it is believed to be completely void, as this is where their concentration is the purest without any imprinting from constellations, planets, stars, or light. All matter that exists around us originates from that same material gathered through forces into different shapes to constitute anything's building blocks. They gather in huge numbers through electro-magnetism and self-magnetism to form the first atoms, which are the main units humans can sense.

At this level, we can start testing what we consider is material. One particle of pure memory is to an atom the earth's size is to our constellation multiplied by around ten quadrillions. The birth of anything is a mere accumulation of these particles at a plethora of levels. The continual accumulation signifies birth and expansion, whereas the death and degeneration are the results of the decomposition and dissociation of these particles back to their single pure memory particle form.

One can imagine all the material and different worlds which exist unseen and untested between the smallest thing we humans can see and these particles. Between us and these particles exists a different larger world to which we are completely oblivious. Thus, our universal knowledge and "all that exists" on our sensical level is only a small percentage of what really exists and is happening in our natural world on this minute level. In this world, all information is shared in this endless memory tissue, stretching in all directions.

The memory associations below atoms remain invisible to us, and what I believe is that animals and creatures with enhanced senses can sense a limited range of vibrations of these associations, while humans lack any such ability. Information flows naturally between all these tissue components; however, our brain cannot read it in its particles form because our minds work on electric signals through electricity, which is a very large number of these particles imprinted many times with different forces to become on the developed level what we can understand. There are no physical and metaphysical worlds in our existence; all is physical irrespective of its size.

The materialization of anything in the world is the direct product of pure memory particles reaching the "still memory" level, where they take their final form. This final form is not still, though; it is where these particles vibrate at different frequencies after being subjected to specific superior forces and energies.

Memory particles are in a constant exchange of information between them at all levels and are interconnected up to the "The Source."

If one was able to see all these exchanges or try to imagine what is occurring, he would understand how fluid our Universe is, both inside of us and outside. As opposed to what it looks like as being still due to the wide spectrum of shading, this memory fills the Universe going from utterly invisible to evident while filling every drop of our existence. Any two memory particles, when they gather, get the first imprinting of each other. Thus, the first exchange of information on the material level occurs. When the right quantity of these particles is joined together, they form the first atom that can now be imprinted with many types of other memories, including genetic memory. Genetic memory is not referred to as memory arising out of our genes but is instead the memory that will form at a later stage, also our genes.

The metaphysical is only beyond our existence or reach. However, what exists is traced of the supernatural in these tiny particles, which could lead us to a little idea of it. What we see, as well as what we do not see, is all material in nature. Traces of the metaphysical before getting imprinted exist powerfully in a lot of these particles. More than half of the material world is unseen to us due to its diminutive size and our limited senses. But what is happening at this minute level up to the atom level is much more than everything combined of what we can see in the whole Universe. There are materials you can never sense or feel and material life you can never imagine, with as many dimensions as you could imagine.

We might not be able to test these dimensions soon due to our sensory restrictions. Also, the fact that our brain cannot process its related information. Unless they are available at a level understandable for us, they become the driving force behind all that exists and everything else we emanate. This is so much out of range to our brain to even comprehend as it is trained on a specific spectrum of sensory information only and can read only electricity, which is a more developed level of these particles by imprinting on several levels. To simplify things, we could see and register about our Universe will never amount to 1% of what it is, as most of it and its components will never be understood or sensed unless we reach the technology needed to watch these particles how they constitute everything in it. In a way, it is a blessing as we would never be able to understand the world to its fullest. The world presents us with a space filled with atoms, molecules, and entities. We would never experience or sense the presence of lesser associations. Unless these particles get in bulk and get imprinted in a sensible way to become atoms, molecules, electricity, etc.., our readings of this world would be minimal and limited. Sometimes, we can feel some very slight unconscious recognition of these particles by our conscious in our body and mind as the electricity still has in them traces of their origin. Still, we do not actually know how to interpret this. It goes unforeseen by disregarding them as we humans tend to neglect whatever has no prior explanation in our minds. This world is not a parallel world, but rather our world where our limitations have been removed.

Our body, heart, and brain, mainly on the unconscious level, can slightly sense the traces of this divine power beyond "The Source" from where these particles originate. Being religious would increase the magnitude of this experience to become faith. Faith is usually a spiritual conviction and feelings. However, the traces of the source are the primary reasons why different faiths came into existence.

From the rudimentary tribes throughout human existence up to our current civilizations, we all believed in a way or another that there is an intelligent driving force that created this whole Universe.

What we can draw from that is what we experience in our life at our human level has a lot of divine in it, even if we do not realize it, before we start imprinting it with all these human sensory memories, by which we do. All our atoms, cells organs are composed of different complexities and associations of this pure memory with divine traces in them and are imprinted on top of our genetic and sensory memories. Therefore, to start searching for what is divine outside of us, we should start looking at the traces of the divine in us, which are closer.

Once one acquires the right mindset and proper understanding of these particles' reality, we would understand that this mega world that seems endless is all formed by endlessly tiny particles interconnected at a minute level. These particles' lifespan is beyond what we know by our time measure and can be considered infinity by our norm as they are not bound by our time, but rather time is bound by them. All existence associates and dissociates from and to them. All get registered into this "pure memory" even if it is unspoken since it exists in your brain, it can be shared across, whether we want or not. Since it is registered somewhere in the Universe, it could be accessed. They are everything and the place where everything gets directly or indirectly formed and created in infinite forms at infinite stages. The Source "pure memory" particles constitute us and all that surrounds us wherever we look. In what we see and what we do not see, the source memory particles are in us and connect us to everything. In this sense, through becoming more aware of the process that runs in us. We can reach anywhere we desire in this Universe. I am not talking physically at this point as to do it, and one needs to dissolve back into pure memory particles again. I am suggesting that we can rather reach by meditating on the information these particles contain and getting synchronized with their frequencies and vibrations. When this level is reached anyone would be able to send information by connectivity means to anything in his environment, as these particles which constitute us, constitute everything around us and link all that exists together. This allows the flow of information between everything.

All Universal laws of whatever nature operate in this context.

Moreover, all that we take as metaphysical, across humanity like, Birth, Death, Ghosts, Angels, Chi, Karma, Laws of Attraction, Laws of Cause and Effect, Sixth Sense, Yoga, Reincarnation, Reiki and everything else of abstract meaning to us, are direct exchanges, associations, and dissociations in various ways of this minute physical world at different levels. Some we create through our thoughts and make them available for use in this tissue of memory and others are attracted to our bodies from it. There is a lot more than this to it for sure as these are only examples.

To put it simply, the memory sent across the source is turned into the frequency and is charged with electricity in our body. The transformed memory plays the role of a magnet attracting everything you wish to act upon. In this minute world of pure memory around you, it will expand across this world in anything you choose to, through these particles. Moreover, the level of magnetism of our actions and thoughts attracts particles and information therein from this memory tissue. We do this all the time unconsciously but applying this more consciously will have a lot of restraints, mainly due to human unfamiliarity with it and limitations. Exchange from you to the outside and from the outside to you through this memory tissue is always running on the unconscious level.

This pure memory in everything in the Universe is for our existence like water is to a fish but are also the fish and are responsible for keeping everything held together at the total level. Gravity which many scientists argue is the main force that holds planets are floating in this memory and everything is being held by it. This could be more explained by simplifying the process a bit to make it more concrete if you get a ball on your outing at the beach and try to hold it up with a grain of sand it will never hold up as the ball is more substantial than a sand particle. Still, if you gather enough sand, the more sand you put, and the more height you would be able to elevate the ball and keep at that height. These particles engulf everything to the extent that there is no emptiness between them. They keep everything, including planets where they are and establish the electromagnetic bond between their totality and what they engulf, which is the same material in different imprinting. The stream of pure memory runs through everything we think exists and non-existing, including the largest constellations and planets to the smallest existing particle and also constitutes through different combinations of their nature. As per our scaling of things a single "pure memory" particle is to one person, what this person is to the whole constellation. They are weightless in our understanding of weight and do travel throughout existence at speeds not even understandable to us from slowest to fastest and vice-versa beyond the notion of place and time that we experience.

Directing all our thoughts towards "The Source" to access it, requires a lot of stillness, focus, and concentration. Meditation and Yoga can have similar effects, but more importantly, stillness is required to get our bodies and minds to be at their lowest frequencies to allow this exchange of free particles through electricity. This renders the electric exchange become at its peak by removing all genetic or sensory interference or lowering them to the most possible. Body and mind purification achieve this task of lowering genetic and sensory interferences. It is essential before consciously undertaking this endeavor to reduce all outside and inside interventions with it. When all these constants gather, it allows us to reach the proper amplification level needed to feel a tiny bit of it and reach a minimal connectivity feeling.

But on the unconscious level, things are different, as we are fully connected to it, and no form of whatsoever nature exists without it. Yet taking it to the conscious level is not easy as it also forms our consciousness, and it requires being highly conscious of your consciousness and unconsciousness at the same time. These pure memory particles are the whole existence in the tiniest possibility ever.

They are the material that runs everything by being the main composure of it on all levels starting from the core level. From what we believe is nothing to the air, the chair, ant, and a single red blood cell, all are composed of trillions of these particles in different forms, different imprinting, and imprinting capabilities.

The "what is not" on our human level, which includes the "what is", and from where desire and action extract and materialize what's in our lives, being thoughts, inventions, experiences, is therefore kept out of reach as fully accessing and reading what is behind the source requires foremost different senses. Still, a clear mind and clear thoughts will allow us little by little to access a part of it through traces in these memory particles, in us and around us, that will allow us to implement the proper mechanism for understanding the basics of being more efficient in this reality and be able to get more productive in materializing all things we look for.

The adequate state of mind to be more aware of this reality would be stillness and calmness as the source and its particles it generates are still and calm in essence. Once someone reaches that state of mind, anything he wishes for can materialize. This is paralleled with a feeling of calm and peacefulness once awareness is reached.

In today's world, it is a job by itself to keep

all this nuisance, pollution and negativity out of our minds so the job would not be easy to go the extra mile, as most people will give up by feeling uneasy in tackling the unknown.

The source's energy is unlimited in nature but limited at the same time when formed. To make things easier, we will compare it to a generator with unlimited power, the more houses this generator provides electricity to, the more the electric power will be limited to each house due to the own house limitation with the electric appliances, electronic equipment, lights, that require power inside this house. Consider the generator powering up 100 houses. You add ten more houses and their appliances to the power load. Each house's power will dim down even though the same power is being supplied through the generator. Therefore, it is a must to keep the maximum number of appliances available to get more use of this energy, especially when it is unlimited and free.

The "Source" is the initiator of the "What is not" which is not seen or sensed by us, which in turn initiates the "what is" seen or sensed by us, and the "What is not" of creation is the most still form of existence, as it is the less congested with imprinting. Let us take the example of the generator again; this generator supplies the main power, we see it at the house, as we have the appliances to see it, but in the generator itself where it exists the most, it goes unnoticed to the outside world.

The procedure to reach the "Source" is too simple, yet too hard for us humans as it requires a huge amount of desire, wants, and complete purity of the mind, to extreme levels and earnest conscious devotion of your full body and mind just to it and this is merely impossible. But as soon as one decides to cut-off and reduce the number of outside stimuli and body and mind pollutants, which mess up with our mind and remove the negative program in our subconscious better readings of it are attainable. It is crucial here to mention that on our inner selves, our conscious is to our subconscious as to the "What is" is to the "What is not" on a large scale. The way to access and control information flow depends on the condition of the building in mind. The precise mechanisms to read and receive the information are present in these particles. In the example of the houses supplied by electricity from the generator, the more receptors you put inside the house, the more power you will extract from the main source.

Once the right approach is reached, the unconscious communication and exchange through these free pure memory particles, which used to occur unconsciously back and forth between our whole bodies naturally, minds and hearts become more organized and directed and a little more conscious. Gaining full consciousness about this process is impossible due to the nature of the particles and the limitation of our body and brain. However, fully aware of its existence and working on directing the energy in a certain direction with purity and clearness of mind while showing modesty by becoming familiar with your limitations and implementing gratitude will allow this exchange process to gain much more magnitude and become more productive.

Accessing the source through its pure particle is not a new concept we acquire. To begin with, we already did subconsciously, but the interference of pollutants kept it from us even realizing it. It will stay this way unless we take conscious decisions to act upon it. It is a simple constant electromagnetic mechanism that already connects us to the Universe and can read in our mind and brain through electric signals. The depths of our thoughts determine how much of the source memory we can retrieve or how little. When consciously aware of this, just thinking about accessing it generates electrical charges and frequencies that consciously connect one's whole body through particle exchange. All of us can master to a variant level this energy and the process of retrieving knowledge from information available in memory around us up to its source.

This pure memory contains the memory of all existence as well as memory stored after creation as memory commutes from and to it and is never lost. What could be lost is imprinting. The process is dependent on your full devotion, concentration, and awareness of it. The longer you would be able to meditate on it, the more you can feel it in your heart first and synchronize your heart feeling with your thoughts, for it works across our body at varying degrees. Electricity generated in our brain can be transcended through frequency and vibrations within these particles to the source, and one can extract through thoughts and electrical magnetism information and ideas from the source.

The brain and heart diffuse electricity in the body and other organs and are circulated across. The heart's right atrium has a major role in generating electricity through the senatorial node; therefore, it also has a major role in the process. The power circuit and generated electricity on cellular and mental levels combine to form the frequency to function on. The frequency is entirely controllable, easy to direct toward tasks, and determines the characters and personalities. The higher your body frequencies, which determine its vibrations, the more mentally unstable and irritated one becomes, and this reflects directly on his personality. This high level of frequencies generated in what I think a higher electrical supply to the brain leads to over jamming it. That is the reason all mental illnesses are possible to be divided and classified by criteria. The range of frequencies from lower to higher determines how severe is the mental issue and diagnoses it based on the symptoms each frequency generates.

How efficiently one could access the source consciously relies on his body's adequacy to attain the lowest vibrations possible to generate the necessary satisfactory frequencies. Our body is like a projector. A projector receives electricity and emits light.

One will not be able to access the source unless he realizes that he and his brain are separate entities and that the brain is only a part of the whole body that needs to be given directions and channeled appropriately into working efficiently. The brain should be thoroughly mastered and not just used on specific occasions. It must be shaped and maintained all the time for it to work correctly. One should befriend his brain and exchange ideas with it, and let his heart, which is another part of our body, be involved in the process. Our heart is our second biggest reservoir and reader of memory. This new consciousness will allow you to open the two main doors to access the source. The brain alone is insufficient for this process as it contains fragments of contamination as you go through purification, i.e., impaired judgment, limitations, or other sensory limitations that have been imprinted in before. The process includes synchronization, combining your thinking process with your feelings and intuition, so you just know it is true when you experience the truth.

This process of experiencing "the source" runs across all existence and is a cycle between us and our environment, but unless you control its outcomes, you cannot benefit from it but at the genetic level. At this moment of frequency exchange, one little by little starts to feel that something is adding up inside and starts getting more familiar with the way it operates.

Electricity is the major player in the whole process as it will activate the memory in our body and turn them into vibrations and frequencies that contain the pure memory particles. Free particles cannot be sent by us unless sent by us in bulk by these two means. We receive vice versa, vibration, and frequency at the source and in our environment by decomposing in our body into particles through electricity. These channels work as such.

This channel should be kept clear, and that is why all mind pollutants should be removed from your life, both body and mind, as they interfere directly in the process of converting electricity in you into the frequency needed to access the source.

So, keep relaxed, get the flow going, joke a lot with a sense of humor, look at your problems, and smile. Your body fluids, cells, and hormones will regenerate and work as they should be.

This pure memory at the source is intelligent in nature. It can be modeled by any means imaginable, primarily by different levels of other vibrations and frequencies that exist in the Universe and all around us as it is showered in the "what is not" part of this Universe to keep life on the "what is" part ongoing.

The frequencies obtained from the source, which are turned into lower frequencies in our bodies, will start boosting one's life, and little by little, materialize the actual powers they contain in one's life. It is a life-changing experience as it will create a sensation of joy, happiness, gratitude, peacefulness, and a deep feeling of life being shaped in a way better form. Even one's ability to control his reality would change, giving him modeling power over all what occurs on the inside and outside. Things you consider as disastrous for the future will alter in your favor, coupled with a strong feeling of helping others out of life's challenges, modeling life in a controlled way. Thus, our conscious knowledge about this process is essential as, without it, our unconscious will diffuse this energy in the majority on the cells and organs level as the brain does not show a big need for it as it is not needed as much in our thought process since we are not aware of it and is needed on the cell level.

But conscious awareness of this does not work by itself without the unconscious being as bare ground, as the unconscious is what enables us, first of all, establish the first connection with the source through our cells, organs, whole body, and mind, by creating a balance between the pure memory and genetic memory in our biology and exchange information with it at all times.

Genetic memory, a pure memory particle imprinted with biological information, comes together to form our subconscious mind read by the brain as such. Pure memory contains the memory of the Creator; it is responsible for all vibrations and frequencies necessary for everything to exist. Therefore, "The Source" contains the first formation which ever existed. This Pure memory, through the frequencies and vibrations, is the initiator of all electricity and light which arises therefrom, to create magnetism which leads to the Creation of genetic memory responsible for the Creation of atoms which combine to form sensory memory and, therefore, life and leads to still memory which contains the traces of all the memories contained in each of the previous. These traces are our doors to access the Universe, and they are like residue in whatever is living to stay connected.

To elaborate more on these processes and how "pure memory" progresses from Creation to our state of existence, it would be helpful to refer to the chart which follows, that explains how memory resonates from Creation to become our life and what we experience within it.

Chart showing how memory cells get embossed, formed and associated from the Source to our Level of Existence.

Ultimate Divine Intelligent Memory

Where Pressure generates Pure Vibrations and Frequencies

Pure Memory at "The Source"

'Electricity Formation'

Electricity is formed by Higher Vibrations and Frequencies

(Traces of Divine Memory)

Running Memory

'Magnetism Formation'

Magnetism is formed by Pure Electricity, Vibrations and Frequencies

(Traces of Divine and Pure Memories)

Genetic Memory

'Atoms formation'

Atoms formed by Magnetism, Electricity, Vibrations, and Frequencies

(Traces of Divine, Pure and Running Memories)

Still Memory

'Life Formation'

State of Existence through Atoms associations through lower Magnetism, Electricity, Vibrations and Frequencies

(Traces of Divine, Pure, Running and Genetic Memories)

Therefore, to attain higher levels of existence, we should reverse the process back, but also, higher levels suggest reaching growth in that direction. The first step to implement is starting to dissolve the old memories and habits on the still memory level and consider all that is already acquired so far as negligible, no matter how broad this knowledge is. That will remove the limitations and the framing previously built-in mind and start relying more on the unconscious. Depending on the subconscious is a must, as the connection established with the higher memory limits is already running in there. Noting down all ideas that come to mind and all signals are the best way to do it.

In this, you should not be interfering with the process. Try to correct yourself, be judgmental about what you write, or try to make it look more comprehendible. Without thinking, one should be writing all that comes to mind without any interference in the process. A one-month period would be enough; I believe an ample data sample would have been collected to be able to analyze. Set yourself and do objective scrutiny of what you wrote, analyze your mind programs, and determine the negative and positive impact of those thoughts on setting the direction of growth. Once this is achieved, starting to work consciously on the intruders would be a good thing to do as you would start to correct your subconscious without even knowing it. After a while, one can discover how things change and guess the limits the brain was subjected to.

These limitations are a direct consequence of heavy conditioning boundaries set by everyday thoughts and experiences for a long period. However, breaking the conditioning is a must, and new innovative ways of thinking and feeling should be implemented. Imagine a long piece of fabric produced for an extensive period, which must be unknotted and fabricated all over again; such is the weariness of the goal of implementing newly acquired thoughts.

Limitations are humans' worst enemy because they create false convictions and persuasions that nothing in someone's situation can be done and he is doomed. Whatever we have as knowledge of things and how many we have experienced things, these are partial truths gathered in pieces from the world. They are usually self-limiting and contain a lot of untrueness as they are based on partial experiences and out-of-context scenarios.

A lot of what we believe as true can avail to us as false at a later stage in our lives and this happens a lot in our lives when we think of something as real and discover later that we conceived things wrongly. Therefore, working on our limitations is the real key to get out of the box we have created and locked ourselves in. Getting above these limitations now would unleash a whole new world, where things are calmer and more growth prospects become possible. What is available as knowledge and information out there is unlimited, and what you could feel you know at one point of your life will turn out to be way minimal when you start knowing, as the more you become aware of things, you would realize that you know so little still. Breaking limitations is a major crucial task one should undertake, being the only way to reach higher levels of memories. Once one admits to himself and conceives that what he learned so far can be all wrong, the process begins. Most of our knowledge is conditioning (If/then), and this would keep us restrained to small areas of activities, as it generates a lot of self-restriction in us by creating a variety of negative ideas and feelings, like hesitation, reluctance, fear, and phobias and all these are limits to our true ability to properly operate.

At this point, one could start to realize the importance of having cleared his body and mind from pollutants. Most of the decontamination is to remove the mental and physical restrictions before this endeavor, widening the channel to advance higher and will create and organize proper memory flow, running memory up to the Source's pure memory stage. Now, one has entered the world of vibrations and frequencies, which is a silent word and requires total calmness, the total dimming of all our senses, and a lot of contemplation. Silence is not only a sign of respect in this context but as an attempt to lower your vibrations and frequencies to become on the lower frequencies these higher levels operate on. As a first feeling, one could sense that the three memory levels overlap. They do, at some level, as genetic memory contains traces of running memory and pure memory to greater extents than the still memory we operate at. Still, with a lot of repetition and higher concentration levels, differentiation between each would be possible as feeling the running memory would be a less enhanced feeling than when experiencing the pure memory. Unlike experiencing genetic memory, which is first an internal process and needs self-reflection, as atoms are what is most imprinted in humans, the other memories are more external with internal interferences and need more profound meditation. This would, with time, allow the resistance of our brain and genetic memory to break, allowing deeper reflection on the running memory and a feeling of separation from what is physical in our understanding to reach the pure memory in its primary form ultimately.

It is a step-by-step process and takes longer to accomplish. When you attempt to reach higher memory, you will discover the traces of higher memories in existing memory and start understanding how layered a human is. To conclude, we can say that memory throughout the Universe is the same with different markings and purest forms with lesser markings. Pure memories combine throughout their spread in the Universe in so many ways to create everything. Whilst registering and embossing where they reach without removing the traces of the origin or other subjectivities throughout the way. From its purest form to become the still memory we strive in, it is a very long way and a lot of recordings, so one must get a clear picture of these recordings to conceptualize the pure form to facilitate experiencing it.

Pure memory, when the adequate frequencies are attained, travel at unimagined speeds which are not subjected to time as we know it. Thus, reaching the memory at the Source when it occurs is immediate and would leave anyone in a very deep state of mind and with a feeling of immense gratitude, weightlessness, joy, among others. It is a feeling which cannot be described with words, as it does not belong to the dictionary we know, and that results from knowing that we would be testing the world of unlimited possibilities. The same magnetism, in a reversed mode of frequencies, and vibrations could be used to attract more memory from "the Source". You can either direct this memory through channeling, which is the most effective way. The indirect approach would be through a transition in the environment.

As vibrations, frequencies could not reach the Source effectively in some instances; they must be combined with other frequencies to magnify the effect. Whatever longing you stretch for an extended period and does not seem to materialize, know that transitioning it is the way to make it happen.

Transitioning is when a part of memory leaves a particular atom in the body to join a higher frequency or vibration after it joins effort with other memory particles from other sources to be directed to the Universe; this can be a conscious action. However, it occurs unconsciously in our social interactions in different ways, like in marriage, relationships, working with a co-worker on a specific project. The process includes the transmutation of memory from high vibrations inside the body to lower vibrations outside the body in our environment, combining with other memories. Reverse transitioning happens when we are receivers of such memory. This memory is usually more imprinted but with more immediate results.

This transitioning is what creates around us layers of pure memory and different dimensions at the still memory level, which we sometimes confuse with the pure memory at the Source, especially in the beginning. At this level, the memory at our still levels is pure. Still, with a lot of imprinting with many types of information from nature, people, and our environment, this is what creates life as we know it and connects us to our environment in so many ways. We and our environment and the whole Universe have melted altogether and differentiated only by the imprinting in each.

Human beings constantly exchange memory with each other and the environment. One of these exchanges is the respiration process, which involves inhaling oxygen and exhaling carbon. However, we never pay any heed to the process. It involves atoms of pure memory when inhaled and exhales back the same atoms combined with memory toxic to our body. Cells are replaced in our body to build new cells through different memory particles and get rid of the old pure memory particles of the cells dying off and turning to pure memory again. This unlimited exchange of memories is the basis of existence in the whole Universe. This memory's shape makes its complexity, vibration level, the amount of memory present at a certain place and its magnetism. That allows memory to bind together, resulting in a human, a tree, a dog, or a table. Therefore, this is crucial in getting how this transmutation is an integral part of reaching and connecting through higher levels of memories and frequencies until reaching the pure memory at "The Source".

The big picture is a big unseen web that surrounds us, full of different types of atoms and free memory in unlimited amounts around us that go unseen, unfelt at most shades, and remain non-existent in us unless we become aware of them. This web that humans, all elements, other atom gatherings are all made of and in constant cyclic exchange of memory with is life running through everything, us, the air, animals, our environment, and the unseen world this memory. It is a circle that models everything and that we can also model if we get more conscious of it.

Remember the army of trillion cells and particles within; currently, you are managing them all on different levels while working on boosting and directing them. So, now would be the time to let all this memory boost run in unlimited power in the direction you have set.

SIX

LETTING THE RIGHT "MEMORY" RUN OUR LIFE

OUR LIFE, OUR actions, our feelings are all operating on a different level now. The unconscious mind is registering new supplied memories and information contained therein, based on a filter now, created by our consciousness which lets all that is not needed out and provides us with a higher form of energy of more pure quality. The adequate memory for proliferation is being added and stored throughout our entire body and our life. This change of vibrations will create a new level of awareness of ourselves and our environment. The power and the effectiveness of this new fresh memory will be reflected as a feeling of serenity for the remainder of our life, where we can genuinely feel the power behind

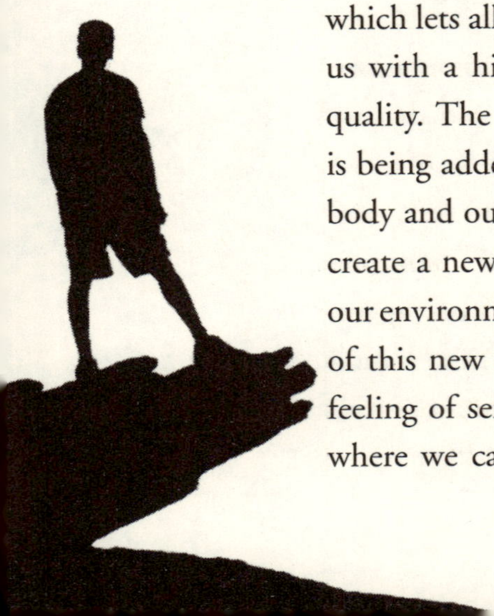

it managing everything. One would find at this stage that he can function better physically, emotionally, and spiritually. Our sense of this force that we gained will educate our soul, spirit, body, and mind to transcend the physical reality we used to experience to another dimension of physicality. A lot of what used to matter in our lives before will matter no more. We now have gained a sharp, deep focus on more crucial things that our conscious or unconscious neglected for a long time in the past. Life will look so completely different from this new reality angle now.

This pure energy obtained from extracting untainted energy from the source will give us more capabilities and new powers to lead a life headed towards prosperity and well-being. One can experience the innate tendency of feeling abundant grows, and our problems decrease in severity, enabling us to solve problems with logic and pure energy. Fear, worry, hesitation, and uncertainty will have no place in our life. One can learn at this stage that our energy can reduce these feelings we always had to a very minimal level and that our thinking process can now kill these feelings in our minds as soon as they are born. Positivity will start to prosper inside, leaving a feeling of constant rest. That would be a life-changer for anyone as he will become a better version of himself. Both body and mind will be synchronized, and all organs and cells will be working on the frequency they should be working on to run properly. One would start feeling rejuvenated and would start noticing not falling sick as much as he did before. It is when our body's ability to heal itself shoots up, and if we already suffer from any health issues, we could realize that disease is controllable, and we can easily fight it with our newly gained energy very effectively. People have beaten many deadly diseases efficiently, just based on faith and belief alone, and faith is only channeling "The Source" memory to the body cells, thus, a small part of the process we undertook. What heals is the energy we are acquiring and not the way we are developing it. Pure memory is positive and carries the intention of the creator. Therefore, being mindful of it and channeling it properly to our body is a daily task we should endeavor to maintain, to keep proper mental and physical health. Consequently, thankfulness and positive thinking are a must as they allow us to keep the flow going with adequate frequency and vibration levels. These are the frequencies to attain a certain level of consciousness to establish a connection with the origin. However, the quantity and quality of pure memory one put at use all rely on the state of mind on which he maintains his body and mind, and what he subjects them to, and therefore this is why purifying our body and mind from all pollutants was essential to be able to attain these frequencies but what is more important is succeeding in upholding this for good.

The placebo effect that we referred to medically at the beginning of the book is so strong because it relies on just this process, which lets our mind unleash the powers within our genetic memory in an unconscious way. When we direct this newly acquired energy inwards, we will soon realize how everything is in our hands and our control. Moreover, we will also realize that we hold a variety of both; directable and redirectable powers towards our environment or ourselves. Thus, the ability to alter our reality would become clearer, and control over modeling our reality would be whole. We can now look at our work and enhance it, at people, and gain their trust and support and at "The Source" to obtain all the energy we require and get back signals from everywhere that we can read. Our sixth sense and gut feeling will be accurate greatly and will be felt strongly. This is where all universal laws that were drafted to regulate all this existence would start to materialize and work in our favor as we are now fully aligned with them. This would allow the proper manifestation of anything we desire. It surely will never be a push of a button or a magic stick, as a lot of building needs to be done little by little within us, but we will realize that everything is lined up in a way that we would be able to do it and that we are on the right track with this sense of accumulation. This is the first block in building our new life. We might have wondered for a long time before why things do not work the way we want them to, but now we actually can realize why and that it was always because of us. The machine which was operating for these things to be happening was fully defective, and a defective machine could never produce a good product.

This newly acquired energy emanating from our newly revealed memory should be released everywhere internally as well as externally, and we should start living it and breathing it and feeling it all the time in full silence, running through our full body and realizing its magnitude would be an experience by itself. We should treat this feeling as our closest silent friend, and it will start giving us clarity throughout our life and let us put sharp boundaries between what is right and what is wrong, between what should be done and what should not.

I suggest that one should turn inside and have a deep conversation with himself at this very stage. Once someone has experienced a conversation with himself, there is no going back. He will realize it's worth and essence instantly.

This positive flow of memory from the source toward our inside and the way we deflect it towards the outside should be protected like protecting one's child and should be watered continuously to become permanent through repetition.

Subjecting one's senses to positive stimuli would be vital at that point to start noticing all the beauty around us. One will discover at this stage that the most beautiful things are kept in the minor things and the simplest matters. This keeps the flow of this pure memory ongoing, and even if its levels get low, the lowest it gets is still a pleasant feeling to have. Once the flow of outside in and inside out is established, one will find himself directing this energy to real goals in his life.

This flow will allow him to focus on major things that he always chose to keep dormant and remove all fears or hesitations that might have held him back before. The surge in energy galvanized by pure memory empowers us to draft the right vision to direct the efflux of energy towards something valuable and more important. Good habits will become a daily routine, and one should feel that this once shattered person here, and there is back whole again.

The good thing about this energy is that it carries persistence, devotion, commitment, and strength, which we all need to undertake anything fruitful, like a certain project to begin.

This ability to see a finite vision for life would become a good addiction and the basis of a more fruitful path that we will be hooked to and seeking on living as per this new arrangement of thought and energy levels. Some days, we could wake up feeling low on this energy. I believe this is because our subconscious mind is still not thoroughly purified of old energy and due to genetic memory, but for as much as needed and especially in the beginning of your "New You" journey, maintenance of this energy and its flow that is done daily should allow us to recalibrate quickly. Some days could pass, feeling the constant need to spend the whole day lifting oneself. Still, little by little, one can discover that the earlier in the morning he wakes if the adequate time to do so is spent, his whole day would have much different results, and the time needed for the uplifting experience is drastically reduced as he will be able to maintain a good feeling throughout the day with minimal input.

Maintenance of the flow is done by restricting all stimuli from interfering with our state of mind. The only way to achieve this is by having a moment of silence and by affirming to ourselves how great life is by self-reminding that everything needs patience and appreciation.

To do so, one needs to feel a connection by heart. It has to be genuine, and it has to be felt deeply. Some motivational and uplifting videos can also help elevate our mood. Once one succeeds in reaching this vibrational level again, his day will be set to run on this frequency flow, irrespective of the events that happen to be good or bad.

The frequency and vibration reached will start determining one's faith by the voltage this experience generates at the atom and molecular levels and the way everything is now aligned and all focused on achieving a certain set goal which is first happiness and prosperity. Productivity will increase, and minor inconveniences that once played a major role in one's life will vanish. Therefore, our achievement and success would be guaranteed, and we could use this technique to achieve anything we desire and manifest all that we look for. This is the real trigger to successfully attract peace of mind and abundance to our life. There is usually a real misconception about how universal laws work or how they are put into effect, which traces these laws to just showing a genuine desire or belief in one's mind, and the Universe will create and provide what is believed or asked for. Still, after getting familiar with these laws and through experience, one could discover that this concept of thinking and focusing on things to get better is very limited in nature and is doomed to fail if not kept within a more significant framework. Some laws will not work and do not work for most people because they don't create the proper environment for them to work and do not apply the complete process, which is a complete lifestyle, rather than bits and pieces from here and there. While some laws, like the law of cause and effect, can materialize in fractions of a second, laws such as the law of reaping and sowing imply seasons, so does the law of attraction and many other laws. However, there are a few laws I do not believe in.

For instance, the law of duality or polarity, as I believe these are created at our "skill level," reflects our life's good and bad conceptualization while life is directed towards prosperity in all means, and only genetic memory renders it unpleasant and hinders it.

Genetic memory is vital as it renders it impossible to have any proper clear image on a defective or broken-down TV, no matter how much we try. We must fix it first and then start adjusting the brightness, colors, and image or movie we want to watch. It is only after implementing the whole procedure of purifying your mind and body and getting rid of the wildness of our survival modes and being able to connect with "The Source" and let the source memory run properly in us, that we can start applying laws bigger than us in our lives and succeed. One should find this balance between him and his environment and "The source" to be able to flourish. All purely rely on the attraction and accumulation of the appropriate nutrients for our bodies, souls, and energies, and to do that, we should become magnets that attract and do not propel.

Moreover, if one's magnet's energy is too low, it would not be able to attract anything. To elaborate this in our context, one must obtain adequate levels of energy from "The Source" pure memory in a purely internal and external milieu and be able to redirect this energy back to "The Source" and to his environment with what he desires for things to work the way he desires. Therefore, keeping our body working on this pure type of memory is crucial.

As soon as we experience this pure memory's imprints, we will learn that all the laws; from the law of Divine Oneness to the law of Vibration, Karma, Cause, and Effect, Polarity, Rhythm, Action to the rights and wrongs are all interrelated and derived from the same energies at different levels.

This is because pure memory particles, which are the only constant in the Universe, are the building blocks of everything in it. It is the constituent atom of all matter and is abided by the same big law, from wood to electricity to humans, and can be partially shifted from an atom to another freely, depending on the ability to understand and deal with it. This memory has the full ability to model or alter any course of action or desire into material things and turn the "what is not" into the "what is" or the "what is" into the "what is not" in splits beyond time or any mathematical equation. Whether for good or bad, whatever we use it for at our level will be magnified to an unlimited scale and would begin to prosper and multiply in and out of one's life. Putting negativity in it is not a good idea, though. Moreover, polluting it with bad imprinting will lower its effects and increase its frequency, so energy will be lost in that vibration. When expressing hate, for instance, this hate, when getting associated with this pure memory, will turn our life into pure misery, and when sent across, it will attract more hate at an uncontrollable vibration level. So, one must be fully aware of what to feel or do because this can be dangerous if used mistakenly as much as it can be beneficial if used properly.

Most of our problems on personal levels or at work, etc., psychological problems, and emotional suffering, when left untreated or unattended, become messes. All problems, illnesses, etc.., are related to one of three issues related to this pure memory when running in our lives. The first being unable to connect to "The Source," and the energy needed for these to subside is not available in our body, and chaos reigns.

The second is the inability to consciously or

unconsciously remove negativity from this form of energy. The third is not knowing how to circulate this energy properly, "the within" or "the without". Once these three issues have resolved any problem, any disease can be sorted out or cured on a personal level as soon as one puts adequate energy and applies an adequate conscious approach towards the problem before the issue gets out of control by the problem or disease taking fully over, where it could be too late.

Running this memory needs a lot of awareness of the fact that atoms in our bodies are already imprinted with genetic memory and rely on the survival mechanism most of the time. This is due to the innate program they run on to preserve our species, and this is where suffering takes place as the change would be going against this wildness in us and try to tame it. Therefore, we would find on that atom level and thus on the cell level and in consequence on all levels an unconscious untamed wolf so aggressive that it attacks any other behavior and tries to either dominate it or run from it by nature. This wolf feeds on the needs of reproduction and being fed. This is the reason why the pure memory at first clatters with it as each is at a different vibration level, but later with repetition, genetic memory is tamed and surrenders to the highest power that becomes its administrator through imprinting.

Once one can discern each memory behavior, hormone secretions in the body will be automatically adjusted, and taming the wolf would be possible to make it work for you.

This process of running on pure memory would result in ruminating part of the unconscious mind into a more conscious state, which could be vaguely read in the beginning to be more explicit with time. One could realize at this level that the unconscious mind consists mainly of all information stored in all atoms of cells and is not a specific part of the brain, but rather the total reading of the brain of the atoms data at the cellular level. This pure memory tries always to control the genetic memory to direct it towards different paths. Knowing that one can start retrieving data from his unconscious to use it consciously by being conscious of how much pure memory is contained in him.

Directing this pure memory particle to reflect a considerable part of the genetic memory it comprises would be a tough job, especially when tackling an area where one could not see due to sensory and mind limitations. But once we succeed in directing our pure memory through repetition and reflecting on revealing genetic memory, a lot of information will start being provided to the brain unconsciously for processing.

A lot of this information would not be understandable to us no matter what we do. Still, a considerable amount of it would form after repetition a certain logic about what genetic memory is but also a small part of what pure memory is through its imprinting of genetic memory and the traces it holds from "The Source".

The unconscious seems to be made of pure memory particles imprinted with genetic memory directly obtained from "The Source" as well as genetic memory imprinting through the accumulation of genetic "survival sensory" memory through generations of evolution on the still level memory at the same time and controlled and kept in order by pure memory. Therefore, our sub-conscious seems to be revealed to us, through two channels, one from the source directly at all times through memory particles exchange and the second from the still memory we inherit and acquire, and this can be an explanation for how life evolves being run by genetic memory with traces of higher memories combined with alternating frequency at the same time. Thus, we, humans, run on pure memory from "The Source" acquired by memory accumulation in our genetic still memory and genetic memory shared by our ancestries at the same time, where other types of creatures that are less complex, as well as all elements, run on only genetic memory with traces of higher memories and are less able to accumulate pure memory directly from "The Source", but mainly traces of it and minor direct source energy. This might explain the freedom of choice humans have not being bound to a set program, but rather two, one which is limited in nature and the second being nearly blank only imprinted by memory from "The Source" that can be imprinted with the choices we select. A tree cannot become but a tree as it runs on only genetic memory on the still level with a program from the traces this memory has from "The Source," so does a dog.

Pure memory particles from the atoms, which form in turn the molecules, which form the cells, which form the organs, which

form us, are all set programs from genetic memory at the skill level, so is our brain. However, the fuel that makes our brain and some other parts operate in the way they do is a combination of the genetic memories, "The Source" pure memory, and the still memory.

That could explain our ability to radiate in return memory particles from the within to the without and to channel these particles back and forth from the without to the within consciously.

As such, the thinking process is an inefficient process by itself if you take it out of this context. On the one hand, if thoughts were not stored, organized, linked together, and grouped correctly, they would not be able to take us anywhere far. On the other hand, if it was not channeled directly to higher memories, it also would take us nowhere as our thoughts would stay on the vertical level only within the framework of still memory where possibilities are minimal. This would intersect with what all religions preach about having a body and soul, where genetic still memory is referred to as the body, and pure memory received from higher memories is referred to as the soul.

CONCLUSION

The world we are living in is a miniature world that mostly we cannot see with a scale going higher for more significant elements' formations. Some are simple, and some are too complex but made of the same base. We have created all kinds of names for the different forms and shapes, but it all gets reduced to one. I do not know whether any living form can see these particles filling around us in its free particles form and have a better sense of it, but I believe if there would also be unseen and non-existent to us.

It is a must, though, irrespective of our ability to see or sense our real world, to keep all our memory particles aligned inside of us. That will allow us to live in the harmony of this particle

world in our Universe, and in us in the purest form possible, to boost our human existence to its unlimited potential and be able to experience our lives in a proper, more organized way.

We are like seeds planted in our environment, from the air we breathe to the people we deal with and have already in use since birth, and through the memory particles, we gather the product of our life experience of what we would become. Thus, one should not spend all his days thinking and wishing and stressing how to become but instead focus on facilitating his growth naturally.

We have the ability at any level, down to our smallest atom, to store more intelligence and more information, whether consciously or unconsciously, and process it by our brain. Never leave a bad memory in you nor around you.

We can have a drastic impact on our past and change it, since it is an accumulation of memory up till the present, by implementing the immediate corrections to what we do not feel at ease with it having happened through imprinting our present memory with better variables, so when the present becomes past through this new addition we have done, it would be a brighter past. Moreover, doing that would give us a more controllable and pleasant approach to our present which we would be enjoying more, and that will inevitably affect our future.

Time as we know it does not exist. Time is only the calculation of the accumulation of memory that leads to a change from the state; it was to the state it becomes. What we feel is time is instead the ultimate organization of memory in the Universe in a precise manner at work.

Prayer by spoken words does not work, as the speech is intended to exchange information through memory particles between humans. Words use sound vibrations, which rely on air particles to travel. Sound does not travel in the Universe where no air is. To speak to the Universe, you need another language, different frequencies, and vibrations than words. It needs what is behind the words you say, the frequencies you emit a real true faith and immense gratitude. Prayer needs to be in silence without saying a single word.

Other creatures in the Universe with more developed brains (memory reader) and more senses, if they exist, and I believe we are not alone as pure memory always develops to reach its still form across existence. There are more complex creatures than us, with more complex reading abilities than we have, and they would be technologically more advanced for sure. Still, we have what is needed, which is a key to unveiling new worlds in an unlimited way.

If we put adequate knowledge into this pure

memory, when it gets imprinted with, it will take us to other levels. It can develop all elements into more advanced creatures with higher abilities and skills.

Life is a severe progression, as we lead it as a fight between genetic and pure memories, but it can be little by little modeled to reach where we want to get in a very smooth way once we grasp the concept of life. Most people suffer for nothing. Suffering and pressure are part of the normal imprinting process, which few only learn to consider as a normal process to change things.

Life is a process of building through hard activities the paths we choose, and it is not accessible if it was easy; everyone would lead a perfect life. Once anyone understands the logic of this journey after suffering for some time, he would realize that suffering is the only way to make the serious decision to stand up and start building his life productively. Hardship is a requirement to push through the memory web.

Re-building requires tearing down the older building to the ground, especially if we have built our life up to this point on wrong foundations. Never fear the destruction phase, as it could be smoother than you can imagine. A sinful life suggests a lot of endless problems, on the financial side of the level of the relationship or any other level. Never run from your old problems when undertaking the new building project. Problems include most of the time, other people. Sit with these people, speak to them and try to reach a solution for these problems to be dismantled. Never consider your problems as non-existent and care less about them as they will surely backfire on you but whenever all that is not needed is destroyed, get back to the building site to continue where you have reached.

One can meditate on destruction and building a bit and see how it follows the same rule of vibrations and frequencies in the Universe. To build anything, we need a certain level of smooth low vibration, but we need a much higher vibration if we want to destroy anything. Contemplate on that in the context of reaching for the Source. Find the right level of vibration, set the right direction for the future, and you will be on the right path to unlock the potentials of life.

Although lousy energy, negativity, murder, chaos surrounds us and control many of us, it is our responsibility to control our lives and direct the results towards organizing it and organizing the memory within. Many people are preoccupied with destruction at many levels due to their ignorance or carrying different agendas emanating from their instinctive genetic memory. But you do not have to be as such as the price could be very high to pay. Chaos does not exist in the Universe around us but rather in people. Even a storm is organized. Our stored memories and what we do out of them on the conscious level determine our life direction and quality. So at least turn them aligned to what is directed and fruitful.

If we do not organize our memory, it will pull us back to the genetic memory level, where instinct reigns to a very great extent. The devil does not exist. We have created him in our lives through our thoughts, feelings, actions, and all other sorts of bad imprinting or lack of imprinting in us and around us and negatively unconsciously programmed our minds and bodies by taking no action to regain control and always expecting a different result. All bad energies, including what we call demons, devils, etc., are created by us, boosting the survival mechanism to its highest and creating our own bad Karma. All this is not available at higher memory levels.

The more we imprint ourselves with negativity and limitation, the more we feel that hell is breaking loose on us and that everything turns against us. Imprinting is Karma. Unconscious negative programming and bad imprinting of memory through bad experiences, bad food, bad thoughts, bad judgments, and bad energy would lead to undesirable effects as we will be facilitating their expansion in our existence, both in us and around us. It is an abyss we unwillingly build due to a lack of knowledge and fall in. So please get out of there and live transparent and straightforward in all this complexity around you.

The whole experience of accessing this Source will lead anyone to a conviction that whatever he thinks, feels, does, and wishes, he becomes.

No matter how important one might see himself, he remains no better at the existence level than everything around him. From the tiniest ant to the largest blue whale, we are all part of the same web. It creates modesty and adds value to life aspects, embedding the idea about real-life values. That will enable you to appreciate the beauty in the tiniest of things, and such values inculcate a practice of living abundantly with less. When one adds value to himself, all good things will get attracted to him, and he will find himself leading a peaceful life in the real sense without even asking for it. Respect people so you can be respected in return and show gratitude to all around you to get it back multiplied.

This book does not suggest that we are living inside a hologram nor software. Still, we are rather living in a big web of existence run by extremely tiny memory particles added to constitute life as we know it and which we can access and alter at any time through electricity in our body and brain to benefit from it at our human level to the highest capabilities. However, most of us choose not to stay in the center, where our comfort zones are. We might not have realized it before, but we have been given custody of an unlimited power consisting of trillions of cells made of trillions of these particles, which we are taking for granted and live life as they do not exist. Unleash this power we have been blessed with into the Universe. Our sadness, madness, and difficult life are the direct results of keeping all this power pressurized inside like a gas bottle ready to explode.

To conclude, I kindly suggest that we look at the memory graph every day and thoroughly analyze it and contemplate it. I do that and discover, day by day, that with all our current technological levels, we were still unable to this point to sense reality as is. It is truly so simple yet too complex and undetectable.

What I fear the most is humans attempting all the time to play with knowledge and reality and try to control it, for I know for a fact that the technology we have could reach a point where we can upload ourselves into a computer to be downloaded somewhere else, we already are currently doing so for some types of memories, which are contained in us.

However, we do not have the technologies to store other types of memory, such as biological memory. I hope we do not tamper with that a lot and keep nature taking its course, at least in what concerns us and our wellbeing. The good news is that, although we can access memory at higher levels and receive a memory from higher levels, no matter how much we interfere as human species with this memory, we are only able to alter things at the still memory level only where all memory reveals itself and where we can only hurt ourselves. This would affect humanity for sure, but the larger picture would still be there unaltered regardless of our existence.

There is no secret to success; there is a system to success where organization and devotion should prevail. Life is a big construction site with pure memory being the whole, so one should start using its constituents of particles to atoms in building proper thoughts and ideas in a systematic way to imprint, impact, and expand what is around him and rely on proper association and dissociation of this memory in a fruitful, productive way. Otherwise, something less effective will be automatically built at the same spot he intended to build. Life is an inclination of memory drives to imprint other memories, so one should shape his life and its stamina in an effective way to start making meaningful imprinting of himself with positive thoughts and actions based on proper knowledge. He should open to change as many of his thoughts and actions need to be altered along the way as he will learn more. No matter what, one should keep pushing in this tissue of life as the more he pushes, the more it will be reshaped in his way and be impacted by his actions.

Remember always that what we put in will multiply and create an impact that will last for a long time until it gets imprinted again, and this will, in turn, create an impact back on the initiator. If, however, one wants to destroy his life, he can take opposite directions and start creating evil, which will multiply in and return to visit him one day. Existence always has a way to correct itself, even if we watch the world today. We can notice a tendency for negativity and evil; it is self-destruction for those who expand it when putting in this equation called life.

Moreover, all the above being said, it is evident that there is an ultimate programmer and designer of all this. We can name God if we deem it proper.

I cannot define him in a single word as all these memory particles that create all that exists and emanate directly from him and are part of him.

Determining what becomes what and how this memory is put together to become existence is a very complex yet organized task. Without such a force, all will collapse. We are made of divine particles vibrating at specific frequencies, so we must try as much as possible to keep it the way it is.

Moreover, this emphasizes the importance of faith in great creative power in our lives and how it puts us one step closer to this divinity, and we try to run from it as we have tendencies through broken knowledge to even run from ourselves.

This book is not a science fiction book. Little by little, one can discover the adequacy in the information contained herein, and science will prove it down the road. Our reality is real but is always a partial reality because of the broken realities that are out there. It is always good to start a big self-review and pinpoint the conditioning we are subjected to.

We are tailoring reality to what suits us best, and this is not real. What fits us is not reality; what fits us is just an excuse we give to validate our ignorance and limitation. Even the mathematical equations we have worked hard to discover and put through humanity are designed to suit our human level, and they are not universally correct. Some might be tailored to facilitate our life but if we take the human element from it, they would be partial. Even 1+1 on our reality level is not equal to only 2 unless we take it to the ultimate truth level: this pure base memory. 1+1 on any other level beyond this basic memory could be equal to any number, including 2, but our partial knowledge makes it equal to 2 regardless of variables.

For instance:

1 human +1 human = 2 humans, thus 1+1=2.

But also 1 human+1 human= 2 heads+2 torsos+4 arms+4 legs, thus 1+1=12 which is also correct.

But also 1 human+1 human = 2 heads+2 torsos+3 arms+ 4 legs, thus 1+1=11 which is also correct if one of them has lost his arm.

Also, 1 human+1 human= 60 trillion cells + 60 trillion cells, thus 1+1=120 trillion, which is also correct if our cells are correct at 60 trillion.

We can keep going on with this formula to reach any number. The number of possibilities for this would be unlimited. Any creature, whether us, a chicken, any matter or element in our existence considering our divisibility on so many levels, whether on the atomic level or on any larger and smaller constituent, we all remain subject to limits. All remains partial and subject to association and dissociation unless we reach the ultimate indivisible unit, the pure memory particle where lies the ultimate truth. However, our thoughts and actions can extend these limits much further than our bodies and environment.

So, work on expanding yourself beyond what you sense, feel, think or see because reality has to it more than you can imagine. It does not matter if you are a doctor, a physicist, a chemist, or a researcher to realize the importance of the shared information. You just need to be a human ready to investigate and analyze.

This book is direct imprinting extracted from "The Source" over a considerable period. The knowledge herein was accumulated in stillness and deep silence. Knowledge is huge and can be acquired once you have the will and the devotion to do so. I acquired some, which I still consider minute, and if I did, anyone could also do it. It is a mining activity, but it is worth the efforts.

All this Universe is one big tree where everything is interconnected by memory exchanges at all levels more rapidly and subtly than even the mind can realize. Hence, at least at the branch level on which we live, let us make it a better place for each and every one of us.

On the last note, if you look in the mirror, you could realize that you are a defined entity with a special appearance as your reflection on it suggests so.

Still, if you mentally zoom in. You could realize that you are divided into smaller parts, being your organs. Zooming in again to realize that you are an even more divided person into cells through this acquired knowledge. Zooming more, you will realize that you are even more divided into atoms. Continuing this process will result in you reaching the true nature of this mini world and sense how particles smaller than anything one can dream of gather to make life. If one meditates on how reality truly is and not what he always perceived, he can then realize that real life is not seen outside, but rather all that lies beneath.

You are You but most importantly the YOU beyond you and made of an unlimited number of smaller than you can imagine matter that not even current most advanced technology can even sense, weightless and non-existent in our norms yet material and total in the existing norms, thus you are a Universe by yourself.

You are a single body with different combinations and shadings of unlimited trillions of life particles.

At this level where the realization comes to your mind, zoom out to all your environment, including its emptiness, and feel it on the same dimensions and levels with all its different shades, then you will be able to apprehend how everything is interconnected at the primary level with different vibration layers expanding out of this base.

Please keep in mind that when this memory fades at our still level as all that associates is doomed to dissociate. And, when this memory is unable to bind anymore together, as the purpose for which it gathered is accomplished and became obsolete.

And when we scatter back in the Universe, back to our original particles untied form. Try to have your memory in its purest possible form as a part of it could join the "Divine Intelligent" memory, and another part would still be present where you make a difference in this world even if you as a defined entity ceased to exist. Try not to leave and leave behind bad memories.

Everything stays, and everything is being kept and registered through imprinting in many forms, even your actions.

WISH YOU PROSPERITY, ABUNDANCE, and PEACE of MIND.

AFTERWORD

"The **YOU** beyond you" needs your attention; it wants you to take care of it. These basic changes necessitate the ultimate transformation of your life. The book is your guide on how to lead the life of tranquility in this otherwise disordered world.

Expanding the vision about the reality of life and being authentic about how we are conditioned to live is what will reveal to us prospects of life never been ventured before. While we all may live in different parts of the world, do different jobs, and work in different fields, somehow, we all are in the desperate lookout to change our lives.

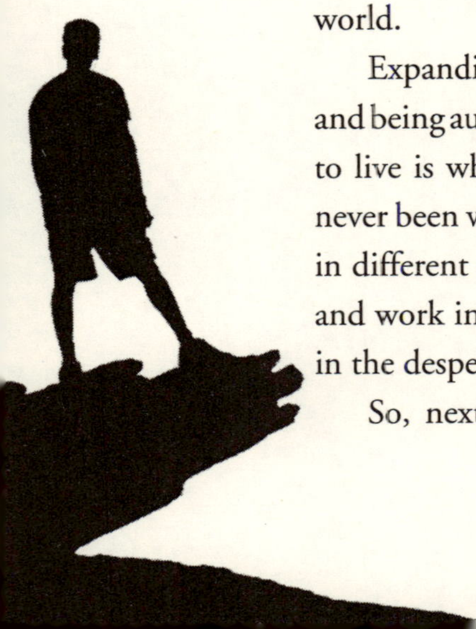

So, next time if someone says "this is how

the world works, stay calm and continue with these changes—the treasure of 'finding the You within' awaits your acceptance and efforts on reformation.

ABOUT THE AUTHOR

Ramzi Najjar is an Award-Winning Author born on July 25, 1978, in Beirut, Lebanon. He completed his college education at Louise Wegmann College and obtained his BA in Political Science and Public Administration from The American University of Beirut. In 2003, he decided to travel to Kuwait after completing his mandatory military service. Through hard work and commitment, he establishes Securita in 2011, one of the leading companies working in the insurance industry today, and later Securita Re in Lebanon in 2018.

AUTHOR CONNECT

GoodReads: https://www.goodreads.com/author/show/20704685.Ramzi_Najjar

Instagram: https://www.instagram.com/ramzinajjarofficial

Twitter: https://www.twitter.com/ramzinajjar_

Facebook: https://www.facebook.com/ramzi.najjar.18

Website: https://ramzinajjar.com

LIST of AWARDS

- Winner of the Literary Titan Silver Award for best book.
- Winner of the Pinnacle Book Achievement Award for best mind, body, and spirit book.
- Finalist in the Foreword Indies Book Awards. Final Results to be announced on June 2021.
- Winner of the AMI Indie Book Award for Best Self-help: Enlightenment Book.
- Honorable Mention in the Los Angeles Book Festival for Spiritual/Religious Category.
- Honorable Mention in the Los Angeles Book Festival for Wild Card Category.
- Winner of eLit Silver Award for the Inspirational / Spiritual Category.
- Winner of eLit Silver Award for the Self Help Category.
- Winner of eLit Gold Award for the New Age / Mind-Body-Spirit Category.
- Winner of the Pacific Book Award for Religious Category.
- Finalist for the National Indie Excellence Awards (NIEA) in the Personal Growth category.